T0347826

BLACK LIVES
Are Beautiful

Black Lives Are Beautiful is a workbook explicitly designed to help members of the Black community counter the impacts of racialized trauma while also cultivating self-esteem, building resilience, fostering community, and promoting Black empowerment.

As readers explore each part of this workbook, they will develop tools to overcome the mental injuries that occur from living in a racialized society. Clinicians who use this workbook with clients will find a practical toolbox of racially informed interventions to aid clinicians, particularly White clinicians, in culturally sensitive clinical practice.

Janeé M. Steele, PhD, is a licensed professional counselor, counselor educator, and diplomate of the Academy of Cognitive and Behavioral Therapies. Dr. Steele is also the owner of Kalamazoo Cognitive and Behavioral Therapy, PLLC, where she provides therapy, supervision, and training in CBT. Her scholarly activity includes service as an associate editor of the *Journal of Multicultural Counseling & Development* and authorship of works focused on the areas of CBT, cultural diversity, social justice advocacy, and counselor training.

Charmeka S. Newton, PhD, is a professor at the University of North Dakota. She is also a fully licensed psychologist and owner of Legacy Mental Health Services, PLLC. Dr. Newton is passionate about mitigating racial disparities in mental health treatment. In 2022, she was honored with the Distinguished Psychologist Award by the Michigan Psychological Association for this work. She is also a peer-reviewed journal author and sought-after speaker.

BLACK LIVES
Are Beautiful

50 Tools to Heal from Trauma and Promote Positive Racial Identity

Janeé M. Steele

Charmeka S. Newton

Routledge
Taylor & Francis Group

NEW YORK AND LONDON

Designed cover image: Nicole Lee and William Lindsey

First published 2023
by Routledge
605 Third Avenue, New York, NY 10158

and by Routledge
4 Park Square, Milton Park, Abingdon, Oxon, OX14 4RN

Routledge is an imprint of the Taylor & Francis Group, an informa business

Library of Congress Cataloging-in-Publication Data
Names: Steele, Janeé M., author. | Newton, Charmeka S., author.
Title: Black lives are beautiful : 50 tools to heal from trauma and promote positive racial identity / Janeé M. Steele, Charmeka S. Newton.
Description: New York, NY : Routledge, 2023. |
Includes bibliographical references and index. |
Identifiers: LCCN 2022047524 (print) | LCCN 2022047525 (ebook) |
ISBN 9781032117522 (hardback) | ISBN 9781032117423 (paperback) |
ISBN 9781003221357 (ebook)
Subjects: LCSH: African Americans–Mental health. |
African Americans–Psychology. | African Americans–Race identity. |
Racism–Psychological aspects. | Social psychiatry–United States.
Classification: LCC RC451.5.B53 S74 2023 (print) |
LCC RC451.5.B53 (ebook) | DDC 616.890089/96073–dc23/eng/20221129
LC record available at https://lccn.loc.gov/2022047524
LC ebook record available at https://lccn.loc.gov/2022047525

ISBN: 9781032117522 (hbk)
ISBN: 9781032117423 (pbk)
ISBN: 9781003221357 (ebk)

DOI: 10.4324/9781003221357

Typeset in Warnock Pro
by Newgen Publishing UK

In honor of my uncle, Russell Hardaway, who was the first to help me learn that Black is beautiful. —Janeé

They never really die they just live on through us. Thank you, Nettie, Leroy, Pearl, Clarence, Mrs. Knox, and Dr. Duncan for living on through me and inspiring me. Your Blackness was beautiful! —Char

Contents

Contents

About the Authors

Janeé M. Steele, PhD, LPC

Photo credit: Van Burch, Sr.

Dr. Janeé M. Steele, PhD, is a licensed professional counselor, counselor educator, and diplomate of the Academy of Cognitive and Behavioral Therapies. Dr. Steele is also the owner of Kalamazoo Cognitive and Behavioral Therapy, PLLC, where she provides therapy, supervision, and training in CBT. Her scholarly activity includes service as an associate editor of the *Journal of Multicultural Counseling & Development* and authorship of works focused on the areas of CBT, cultural diversity, social justice advocacy, and counselor training.

Charmeka S. Newton, PhD, LP

Photo credit: Barika L. Pace

Dr. Charmeka S. Newton, PhD, is a professor at the University of North Dakota. She is also a fully licensed psychologist and owner of Legacy Mental Health Services, PLLC. Dr. Newton is passionate about mitigating racial disparities in mental health treatment. In 2022, she was honored with the Distinguished Psychologist Award by the Michigan Psychological Association for this work. She is also a peer-reviewed journal author and sought-after speaker.

Introduction

Black people are beautiful. You are beautiful. Yet, many of us don't always feel this way and some of us don't even believe this is true. While there are many reasons a person might not feel good about themselves, for Black people, damaging beliefs about self are often connected in some way to the negative, stereotyped messages they've received about their race. We wrote this book to counter those messages and to promote healing from the psychological and emotional harm that comes from internalized messages of Black inferiority.

Over the past few decades, the beauty of Black people and Black culture has become widely embraced, evidenced today through hashtags like #BlackGirlMagic, #BlackBoyJoy, and #BlackExcellence. Yet, the belief that Black is less than beautiful, a notion that dates back centuries, is still with us in many ways. In fact, in the United States, evidence of this belief pervades nearly all aspects of society. For example, anti-Black imagery and stereotypes can be found throughout U.S. pop culture in everything from advertising, to entertainment, to music, to literature. Think about how the maid and butler iconography of products made by Aunt Jemima and Uncle Ben's reinforce the subservient status of Black people, or how the "jive talking" crows in the childhood film *Dumbo* reinforce stereotypes that depict Black people as uneducated and poor. While these are two very specific examples, the reality is that these types of images have been numerous enough to fill entire museums across the country, including the Jim Crow Museum in Big Rapids, Michigan and the Smithsonian National Museum of African American History and Culture in Washington,

DOI: 10.4324/9781003221357-1

DC. While the nature of these images has varied across generations, the messages of inferiority behind them have not. Black is still viewed as less than beautiful not only as it relates to physical beauty, but also in terms of culture and intellectual capacity as well.

The anti-Black messages that pervade U.S. society have had a detrimental impact on the psychological wellbeing of Black people as a community. In particular, beyond the negative impacts of racism in itself, the resulting internalized racism that occurs due to anti-Black messaging has contributed to poor outcomes in the Black community as it relates to education, health, and socioeconomic status (Versey et al., 2019). While some individuals recognize the connection between different forms of racism and social determinants of health and wellness within the Black community, other individuals who are influenced by racist worldviews and biases, whether consciously or unconsciously, attribute the negative conditions that affect quality of life for Black people to personal moral failings, a lack of ambition, low intelligence, or deficits in genetics and biology. From their perspective, if Black people didn't have these limitations, they would be able to "pull themselves up by their bootstraps" and achieve any level of success they desire. This idea, however, goes against something Black people have proved time and time again—that we are fully capable of succeeding and excelling at the highest levels of society. And we do. The subordinate status Black people have been relegated to in society is not deserved, it is not inevitable, and it is not natural (Versey et al., 2019). Instead, the achievement gaps observed in the Black community are much more attributable to systemic barriers that can be difficult to overcome, and at the very least, take an emotional and psychological toll.

The Myth of Race

It's hard to deny the impact race and racism has on the lives of Black people. The process of unpacking this impact and healing from its trauma requires us to first unlearn some of what we've been taught about race. Most individuals are raised to believe that the physical differences we see among groups of people can be attributed to a biological category of human diversity called "race." Yet, research shows that the concept of race has very little scientific foundation in terms of biology or genetics, leading scientists and other researchers to describe the older, more commonly held notions of this construct as "the myth of race" (Fairbanks, 2015).

Many people are surprised to learn that race is not a biological fact, but it's true. Scientists who study genetics say that 94 percent of human genetic variation is found within members of the same race, while only 6 percent of this variation exists between races (Burns & Vaughn, 2021). This means that biologically, people from the same race differ more from each other than they do from people of other races. In other words, two people of African descent may be more biologically similar to a person of European descent than they are to each other. The differences we see in skin color, hair texture, etc. are a result of gradual and continuous adaptations that occur in the human species as we move across geography and climate. They do not correspond to traits like intelligence, athletic ability, or personality.

If this is your first time hearing this idea, you may be asking yourself, "If race is not a biological reality, then where did this myth come from?" The simplest answer to this question is this—essentially, the concept of race was invented during the late 16th century as part of the European expansion into the "New World" (Smedley, 1999). Those responsible for shaping public consciousness at the time—people such as scientists, anthropologists, spiritual leaders, and government officials—used pseudoscientific methods and religious philosophies to create racial hierarchies that would justify three things—slavery, colonialism, and the conquest of people they defined as inferior (Roberts, 2012). For example, in the social sciences it was argued that Africans were heathens, and it was a Christian duty to save their souls by capturing and enslaving them (Smedley, 1997). In the hard sciences, individuals in newly invented fields of study such as craniometry used information like measurements of skulls to assert that Black people had smaller brains than Whites, and were, therefore, less intelligent. These philosophies and scientific methods seem absurd to us now but at the time they provided the moral and intellectual legitimacy needed to start social practices that distribute wealth and value to the people at the top of the racial hierarchy, while oppressing and dehumanizing those at the bottom (Sidanius & Pratto, 1999).

Understanding that race is a biological myth is important for several reasons. Many Black people experience a sense of shame and alienation due to what they believe are inherent, biological deficits in the Black race. For some, this sense of shame leads to deeply destructive attitudes and behaviors such as self-hatred, powerlessness, helplessness, and stress responses like substance abuse and other forms of self-harm (Pascoe & Richman, 2009; Prilleltensky & Gonick, 1996). For others, the internalized shame around being Black leads to an opposite but equally destructive set of attitudes and behaviors, including being overly focused on obtaining material goods and status, conforming to White cultural standards, estrangement from the Black community, and in extreme cases, vilification of the Black community (Schiele, 2005). Realizing that the entire basis for this source of shame, the concept race, is entirely made up can help to free you from any conscious or unconscious limitations you may be placing on yourself based your race. It can also make it easier to develop positive feelings about being Black, which, as we stated earlier, leads to better emotional and psychological wellness.

You Can't Steal Our Joy

So far, we've discussed some pretty heavy topics. For most of us, thinking about these things for too long or too much at one time can be overwhelming. So, we thought it would be a good idea for us to take a laugh break. While the oppression of Black people is in no way funny, we know that as a community we have found comfort through the use of humor and by being able to laugh at ourselves.

Part of the beauty of Black culture is its collectivist nature. We look out for each other and we're good with the ebbs and flows of life. Part of these "ebbs and flows" is a loose conception of time. We thought we'd share a funny take on this from one of our favorite comedians, Bernie Mac.

> When White people go on break at their job. Fifteen minutes. They go to their desk. They eat their cheese sandwich. Drink their God damn tea. Fifteen minutes they're back on the f—ing job. My people, I don't know what the f— is wrong with us. But when we go on break, that's just what the f— we do…we break. You got to look for our motherf—ing ass. "You seen Johnny?"
> —*Bernie Mac*, Kings of Comedy *(Lee, 2000)*

Bernie Mac's comedy, just like that of early Black comedians like Clerow "Flip" Wilson Jr., Redd Fox, Dick Gregory, and Richard Pryor, shows us how we can cope by using humor. For centuries Black people have suffered the distress of racism, but at the same time we have found comfort in being able to laugh. Comedy has become one way in which we break the tension of the racism we experience. It could be argued that we use humor to chip away at the intensity of being Black in America, and humor can be an act of resistance against a system that often excludes and treats us as inferior. Thus, humor is good for the Black soul. So, as you navigate your way through this workbook, we encourage you to extend grace to yourself and even find some laughter, as sometimes there is healing that comes through our laughter. We want to start you on your journey of finding some humor as you engage in your work. The following list gives three comical videos about the Black experience you can find using Google. Again, if you find yourself becoming overwhelmed as you journey through this workbook, take a laugh break as you work to find your joy and beauty of your Blackness:

- ❏ Trevor Noah's *Being Black In America*
- ❏ Kevin Hart's *Guide to Black History*
- ❏ Bernie Mac's *Differences Between Black & White People*

Race as a Social Construction

While advances in the study of genetics have debunked the science behind biological notions of race, race as a social construct nevertheless remains one of the most salient aspects of identity for people not only in this country but around the world. In particular, although race as a biological construct may be a myth, the racism and discrimination Black people face due to the social construction of race is very real. Accordingly, race as an aspect of identity is important because when we deny the existence of race, we hinder our ability to challenge social policies and beliefs that have a negative impact on the development and wellbeing of people who are negatively affected by racism. In order to eradicate racism, we must acknowledge that race and racism exist.

Beyond this, understanding that race exists as a social construction is important because race can be a source of strength. Black people throughout the African diaspora feel a sense of pride and kinship stemming from our shared history, cultural heritage, and contemporary experiences. The term *diaspora* refers to all of the people of African descent who live outside of the continent, irrespective of their citizenship or nationality (African Union, n.d.). We like the term diaspora because it creates an image of Black communities across the world having a feeling of connection and family. So, while race is important because people of color face shared experiences of racism and discrimination, it is also important because it creates a special bond that unites us by our common sense of values and ways of being.

Within races, there are various ethnic groups. According to cultural anthropologists Audrey and Brian Smedley,

Ethnicity refers to clusters of people who have common culture traits that they distinguish from those of other people. People who share a common language, geographic locale or place of origin, religion, sense of history, traditions, values, beliefs, food habits, and so forth, are perceived, and view themselves as constituting, an ethnic group.

(Smedley & Smedley, 2005, p. 17)

U.S. Census Bureau data identifies the most common Black ethnicities in the United States as African American, Jamaican, Haitian, Nigerian, and Dominican. Yet even these distinctions highlight the inexact nature of terms used to define one's race and ethnicity. In the country of Nigeria, for example, Nigerian would refer to one's nationality, while one's ethnicity might be Yoruba, Igbo, Hausa, or another one of more than 250 ethnic groups in the country. While all Black people share similar cultural worldviews and ways of being, there are also differences in traditions, customs, values, and histories among the various Black ethnicities that are important to consider as we look for ways to heal from racial trauma.

The ideas presented in this book reflect our specific ethnic background. Therefore, as you read through the following chapters, you may find yourself relating more or less to the concepts or experiences we describe, depending on your own ethnicity. We are both African American women, born in 1980. Accordingly, our views on race and racism are informed by the experiences we had as African American children growing up in the United States during the 1980s and 1990s. In many ways, coming of age during this time afforded us opportunities to participate in an explosion of what we now call "Black excellence" culturally. For example, during the 1980s and 1990s, the number of Black college graduates and business executives increased exponentially, as did the number of Black entertainers who reached millionaire status. For young African Americans such as ourselves, these signs of upward social mobility helped us to believe that we too could live prosperous and successful lives. If others could do it, we could do it too.

At the same time, the realities of racism continued to plague our community during the 1980s and 1990s, much as they do now, complicating the burdens and difficulties of life. At a broad societal level during these decades, the Black community was experiencing the detrimental effects of racist policies such as the War on Drugs, stop and frisk, and the three strikes law, as well as continued exclusion from some segments of society and entertainment like MTV. While these policies did not affect everybody individually, many people had friends or family members who were affected, and many individuals experienced everyday racism such as racial slurs and profiling in stores and restaurants. We certainly were not exempt from these experiences, as we also encountered racism on a personal level in a way that intimately connects us with the content of this book and created our own need for racial healing. In what follows, we share two short stories to illustrate what our experiences with racism and racialized trauma were like for us as children. Then, in the next section, we share additional stories to illustrate the process of overcoming this trauma en route to developing a positive racial identity.

Dr. Janeé

My story occurs on Christmas Day, when I was around 4 or 5 years old. I had been fantasizing about a Cabbage Patch Doll and when presented with a large, wrapped box from my uncle, I was certain my fantasy was about to come true. Upon unwrapping the gift from my uncle, however, my excitement soon turned to disappointment after opening the box and seeing that while I had in fact received a Cabbage Patch Doll, she was Black. I can remember just sitting there staring at the box, feeling sad. This doll wasn't beautiful like the White doll I wanted, and it didn't look like the kids I went to school with or the teachers in my class. My sadness and disappointment weren't things I could articulate or even understand at the time, but I felt them, nonetheless. Essentially, I thought this doll was less than because it was Black, which was an internalization of the messages I had received at that very early age. Thankfully, as you'll read in what follows, I was able to have corrective experiences that changed the negative internalized views I had around being Black. I now feel good about being Black and see it as a source of pride.

Dr. Char

Imagine being an 11-year-old Black child hanging out with your friends. On a hot summer day, you and your friends enter a convenience store just to buy some snacks, maybe some Skittles or a bag of chips. You have money in your pocket for the purchase, however, upon entering the store you and your friends, who also happen to be Black, are followed from aisle to aisle by the White store clerk who because of her racism has stereotyped you and your friends as being thieves and unsafe for being in her store. Once you realize what is going on, you put back your purchase and leave the store.

Unfortunately, this story is not fictional. This was my reality as an 11-year-old and was perhaps one of the first times I realized that the world was not always a safe place for Black kids like me. I remember feeling hurt, confused, and angered by the situation. I remember leaving the store and telling my mother about the experience and her working to explain racism to me and how to handle these situations. As I got older, these race conversations became a topic of frequent discussion in our home. My parents knew they had to protect their children from a world that was quick to treat them as inferior. This impacted me so much to the point that now as an adult and decades later I still remember that experience and the hurt.

Racial Identity

While the experiences shared were emotionally impactful for us at the time of their occurrence, each experience had different significance in terms of its contribution to our overall racial identity. *Racial identity* refers to an individual's sense of belonging to a particular racial group (American Psychological Association, n.d. b). Beginning in childhood, individuals are exposed to various messages that influence the development of their racial identity. In the United States, these messages tend to assign a level of superiority to Eurocentric beauty and cultural norms, while simultaneously portraying the beauty and cultural norms of other racial groups as inferior. Black children, for example, receive messages of inferiority when they hear racist language on school grounds, are underrepresented in academically talented school programs, and receive negative feedback about their hair texture and styles from peers, and in some cases, official school policies. The sadness and disappointment Janeé felt after receiving her first Black Cabbage Patch Doll reflects this sense of inferiority and is consistent with research which shows that by age 4, children in the United States ascribe a higher social status to White individuals and associate people of color with negative traits (Sullivan et al., 2021). Although Janeé, like other children of this age, had not actively begun the process of forming a self-defined sense of identity, the budding shame and alienation she associated with being Black became background noise that had to be overcome later in life once she did begin to crystallize her view of herself as an African American woman.

Char's experience, on the other hand, represents the type of encounter that typically shifts race out of the background and launches individuals into active racial identity development. *Racial identity development* refers to the process through which individuals develop a healthy view of: (a) themselves, (b) members within their racial group, and (c) members of other racial groups (Constantine et al., 1998). One of the most popular models of Black racial identity development was first established in the early 1970s by psychologist William E. Cross, Jr. In the decades since its initial development, Cross's model of Black racial identity, often referred to as *the nigrescence model*, has become one of the most popular and widely researched models of Black racial identity development. Using this model, psychologists have been able to identify the emotions, thoughts, and behaviors individuals exhibit as they resolve negative feelings about being Black and develop a positive view of themselves as racial beings. Understanding the stages of Black racial identity development for yourself can help you to assess your own level of racial identity. It can also help you to identify areas for future growth.

According to the nigrescence model, the process of becoming accepting and affirming of a Black racial identity begins during adolescence for most individuals and continues throughout adulthood (Vandiver et al., 2001). Prior to adolescence, most children are in a pre-awareness state relative to their racial identity. During adolescence, however, teenagers enter a stage of human development where they begin to understand and define themselves with reference to important social groups outside of their families (Tatum, 2017). At the same time, teenagers are also beginning to have racial encounters that spark greater recognition of the "common fate" or "shared destiny" they have with other members of their racial group, which triggers active examination of what it means to be Black (Tatum, 2017; Umaña-Taylor et al., 2014). The combined effect of these milestones is illustrated in Char's story when as an 11-year-old she was forced for the first time to really reckon with the role racism and discrimination would have in her life after being racially profiled at a local convenience store. For Char, like countless other Black teens before and after her, this reckoning propelled her beyond the passive absorption of dominant culture's norms and beliefs into an active examination of what it means to be Black. Essentially, Char began the process of challenging the Eurocentric worldview she was socialized into as a child, progressing through stages of the nigrescence model: pre-encounter, encounter, immersion–emersion, and internalization (Vandiver et al., 2001). These stages are reviewed in greater depth as follows.

Pre-Encounter

Pre-encounter is the first stage of Black racial identity development, according to the nigrescence model (Vandiver et al., 2001). For individuals at this stage, the concept of race is characterized by either low or negative salience. *Salience* refers to the importance of race in a person's life. It can range from low to high and be positive or negative. This means that at the pre-encounter stage, individuals can have either an *assimilation identity*, where race has low importance and little personal significance, or an *anti-Black identity*, where an individual has been miseducated and as a result believes negative stereotypes about Black people, or worse, internalizes these stereotypes to the point that they develop a sense of hatred for both themselves and Black people in general (Vandiver et al., 2001).

Individuals with an assimilation identity typically adopt pro-American or mainstream values and give little conscious thought to the role of race in their lives (Vandiver et al., 2001). These individuals assign a higher status to mainstream norms such as White hairstyles and dress, use of standard English, and belief in the "pull yourself up by your own bootstraps" concept (Endale, 2018; Katz, 1985). They also tend to prioritize status and power obtained through credentials, titles, positions, and economic possessions. Char, for example, grew up right off of the infamous Eight Mile Road in a small predominantly

Black suburb of Detroit called Oak Park. During her childhood, Char did not experience much cultural diversity, as the majority of her classmates were African American. Those who weren't African American belonged to a small population of Middle Eastern families in the community. In line with an assimilation identity, race was not a very salient factor for Char. In her case, this was due to being encapsulated in a predominantly African American community. Nevertheless, the socialization she received through avenues such as TV, the news, and school textbooks resulted in a desire to achieve a level of success she associated with White culture, as well as a belief that her personal efforts would guarantee her passage into that culture. Accordingly, Char worked hard to succeed and present herself in ways consistent with the mainstream. Being Black didn't start to have salience for Char until she began to have race-based experiences like the encounter at the convenience store.

Janeé's early adolescent experiences, however, are more illustrative of an anti-Black identity. Janeé grew up in a racially and ethnically diverse suburb of San Francisco called San Mateo. While the city and its schools as a whole were diverse, its neighborhoods were racially and economically segregated. As a result, the messaging Janeé received about White superiority and Black inferiority was more direct. For example, at the elementary and middle schools Janeé attended, Black students were, for the most part, underrepresented in extracurricular activities like Girl Scouts, as well as in academically talented programs. Beyond the structural racism evidenced in the exclusion of Black students in extracurricular and gifted programs, interracial friendships among peers were also tenuous and predicated upon an unspoken pro-White bias. Many of Janeé's most vivid childhood memories surrounded these aspects of her grade school experience. In 6th and 7th grade, Janeé had a close friend, Alyssa, with whom she often spent lunch breaks and exchanged letters. During one passing period in between classes, Alyssa gave Janeé a letter in which she had drawn a picture of Janeé with the word "turd" and an arrow pointing to Janeé's short, braided ponytail. The girls were friends and Alyssa meant the comment as a joke; yet the letter triggered a deep sense of shame and humiliation in Janeé. While an anti-Black identity often reflects a conscious disdain for Black cultural norms and aesthetics, it can also be characterized by an unconscious sense of low self-esteem stemming from internalized racism. This state of low self-esteem and internalized racism is where Janeé found herself as a 12-year-old who was indoctrinated into an ideology that prized White beauty and demeaned African phenotypes and hair textures.

Encounter

The second stage of Black racial identity development is known as the *encounter stage.* The encounter stage occurs when an event or a series of events leads to an increased awareness of the meaning of being Black and triggers a change in pre-encounter identities (Vandiver et al., 2001). For many individuals, these events take place within the context of personal experiences and observations, education, or activism (Neville & Cross, 2017). Most often, *personal experiences and observations* refer to direct experiences with racism and discrimination or witnessing racism and discrimination. *Education* refers to formal or informal education about the history and cultural experiences of various groups of Black people. Formal education includes things like taking university courses or participating in community-based workshops, while informal education refers to things like travel or independent reading. Finally, *activism* refers to participation in activities such as advocating for changes in laws and unjust social policies, capturing social injustices on film or video, and protests (Neville & Cross, 2017).

A main outcome of events occurring at the encounter stage is the experience of a racial awakening (Neville & Cross, 2017). This awakening occurs due to growing a critical awareness of what it means to be Black in a racially hierarchical society, something Char often describes as a "rude awakening." After graduating high school, Char decided to go directly to college but was undecided as to what college to attend. While participating in a new student orientation for one of the schools she was considering, she sat down with an advisor who happened to be White and another incoming student who also happened to White. As the advisor began to help both students select courses for the Fall, Char noticed that the advisor was quick to enroll Char into 099 remedial courses, while the White student was enrolled in regular level courses. Concerned about this, Char asked why she could not start off with 100 level courses, to which the advisor replied, "Well, you know we want to make sure we get your GPA high starting off and we want to make sure you succeed your first semester." Char was confused by the advisor's response. Had he not seen her transcripts and known that she had a 3.8 GPA? Did he not realize that she had taken and passed advanced placement level courses and had graduated seventh in her high school class? As Char sat there with the advisor and the other student, she began to question if she had been stereotyped because of her race. And while she did not end up attending that university, the experience of having her intelligence questioned and her voice unheard was felt throughout the entirety of both her undergraduate and master's level studies. During her studies, curriculum that was devoid of diversity, along with a lack of racially diverse professors, touched Char's inner thinking, spurring her to re-evaluate the relationship between Black and White people in American society.

Janeé's encounter events, on the other hand, were primarily characterized by education and activism, which was, in part, due to family values around reading and the tradition of activism in the Black church. Janeé was raised in a family of avid readers. When she was around 10 years old, the same uncle that bought her the Black Cabbage Patch Doll also bought her a book called *Lessons in History: A Celebration in Blackness* by Dr. Jawanzaa Kunjufu. In the book, Kunjufu (1987) discussed topics such as the size and significance of the African continent, the beauty and functionality of Black skin tones and hair textures, and accomplishments made by Black people such as George Washington Carver, Langston Hughes, and Mary McLeod Bethune. While receiving this book was not enough to completely shift the anti-Black bias Janeé unconsciously held, the ideas presented in Kunjufu's (1987) book were like seeds that eventually began to grow as Janeé became immersed in the fertile grounds of cultural experiences that honored and celebrated Black culture, many of which were attended as part of her church youth group.

Immersion–Emersion

After individuals encounter events that lead to increased awareness of their marginalized racial status, they subsequently enter a phase of Black racial identity development known as the *immersion–emersion stage.* According to Vandiver et al. (2001), this stage represents a period of life when individuals begin to embrace Black culture and enthusiastically seek to learn more about Africa and African Americans. Accordingly, one aspect of the immersion–emersion stage, referred to as *intense Black involvement*, is characterized by a voracious consumption of Black art, literature, and history, as well as increased participation in historically Black organizations and social institutions. A positive aspect of this intense Black involvement is the development of an internalized sense of pride concerning one's membership in the Black community; however, individuals at this stage also frequently experience feelings of rage and even guilt as their eyes become open to the atrocities that have been perpetrated against the Black community, leading to another aspect of the immersion–emersion stage known as *anti-White attitudes* (Vandiver et al., 2001). While these attitudes may be negative toward White people and White culture, they are more often than not the result of anger toward society for the oppression of Black people, as well as anger toward oneself for having previously ignored or downplayed the role of race in one's life, and are typically transformed into more egalitarian ideals as individuals move into the final stage of Black racial identity development (Vandiver et al., 2001).

For Char, intense Black involvement and anti-White attitudes began while pursuing her doctoral degree in counseling psychology. During her doctoral studies at Western Michigan University, Char encountered several Black professors who really helped her to embrace her Black racial identity. At a basic level, the simple act of seeing those professors excel at that level in higher education was inspirational to Char and helped her to believe that she too could be a successful psychologist and professor. Beyond being an inspiration, the Black professors in her department also served as a source of wisdom and support, as they frequently celebrated her accomplishments, advocated for her with other faculty in the department, and gave her advice concerning how to navigate the field as a young Black professional. Two professors in particular, Dr. Lonnie Duncan and Dr. Joseph Morris, frequently discussed with her the importance of not only empowering and educating herself but going back into the community to empower other young Black psychologists as well. Likewise, the other Black students in her department also served as a source of support, as they regularly organized social events where the Black students in the department could play games and have a safe space to vent about difficulties with racism and just feel a sense of community and connectedness with one another. Like most individuals at this stage of Black racial identity development, Char psychologically and physically withdrew into Blackness and a Black world as she soaked in the love she received from the Black people around her. At the same time, she also recalls having heated arguments with White colleagues around issues of multiculturalism and race. In particular, she had a low tolerance for White Americans who did not own or accept their privilege. However, as typical in terms of progression through Black racial identity development, Char eventually transitioned into a more balanced view of Blackness which included letting go of some of the anger she had toward White people as she read and had experiences which taught her that anger was a dead end, yielding little productivity.

As previously mentioned, Janeé's intense Black involvement began earlier in life than Char's, as Janeé was given an explicitly pro-Black education by relatives and her church not only through books and other formal means of education, but also through immersion in activities that celebrated Blackness. Throughout adolescence, Janeé was fortunate enough to have adults in her life who regularly took her to participate in various marches, protests, and Black cultural events. Janeé remembers with pride being featured in her local newspaper as a teenager for participating in her community's annual MLK march and being encouraged and fortified each summer and winter after engaging in yearly Juneteenth and Kwanzaa programs with her church youth group. Psychologically, Janeé was also affirmed by both Black and White peers for her dark skin and hair texture, which further contributed to a sense of confidence and pride in her Black racial identity and encouraged her to embrace Black fashion and beauty aesthetics. For example, Janeé regularly wore a gold Nefertiti necklace gifted to her by one of the women in her church, purchased Fashion Fair makeup, and sported clothes with pro-Black slogans and African designs. Still an avid reader during her teenage years, Janeé was also a consumer of Black magazines like *Ebony*, *Essence*, *Jet*, and *Vibe*, as well as books that delved into historical and contemporary African American experiences and were written by Black women such as Terri McMillion, Toni Morrison, and Alice Walker. While fashion choices and reading preferences may seem trivial in some regards, for Janeé, these parts of her life reflected an overall resistance against assimilation into dominant culture and a shedding of the anti-Black attitudes she had been indoctrinated into as a young child. Anti-White attitudes were a lesser part of her identity during the immersion–emersion stage, as she maintained close friendships with individuals from multiple racial groups, including some White women with whom she remains friends today.

Internalization

The final stage of Black racial identity is known as *internalization*. At this stage, individuals view their Blackness with positivity and have an overall sense of comfort with themselves as racial beings (Vandiver et al., 2001). This greater sense of comfort and self-acceptance is often accompanied by a shift from pro-White to pro-Black attitudes that result in changes to their overall worldview and values (Vandiver et al., 2001). For example, for some individuals at this stage of development, the attitudes reflected in their worldview and values are characterized by a prizing of Afrocentric principles in what's considered an Afrocentric of Black Nationalist identity (Simmons et al., 2008). For others, this shift in ideology may be more bicultural in nature, where being Black and having another marginalized identity such as being a woman holds salience, and for yet others, identity at this stage may focus on accepting and valuing all other cultural groups in what is considered as a multiculturalist identity (Worrell et al., 2001).

For Char, the more she began to study her own identity and the more dialogues she had with Whites professors in the classroom, the more she started to realize that not all White people were "bad." In fact, some White people are allies. This realization led to greater control of her behavior and intense emotions around race-based issues when participating in dominant society, having developed a greater sense of calm and ease. She was also able to feel a little bit more empathy for and acceptance of White people. In terms of her worldview and value system, her positive sense of Blackness has led to a general sense of commitment to the concerns of Black people as a group, which has been sustained over time. For Char, this commitment has included engaging in activism, providing voice, and offering mental health services to marginalized members of the Black community, as well as training and educating others about issues around race and racism. As a new mother, it has also included helping her son to develop a positive racial identity by sharing books and messages affirming who he is as a Black man.

Finally, for Janeé, the internalization stage has been characterized by a continual focus on *self-actualization*, or in other words, acceptance of a positive Black identity and improved psychological functioning and self-concept (Vandiver et al., 2001). This has included continuing her education on the Black experience and the psychology of the Black experience, as well as use of the knowledge gained through this education to observe and challenge unconscious remnants of her own internalized racism and poor self-concept associated with being Black. For example, through her research on issues such as imposter syndrome, racialized trauma, and deservingness, Janeé has learned to pay attention to physiological signs indicating when these issues may be at play in her life, and to extend herself grace, self-compassion, and self-acceptance in response to these moments instead of self-criticism and self-doubt. And like Char, Janeé has also dedicated significant portions of her professional and personal life to educating others and helping to mitigate the impact of racism on the lives of all individuals affected by this phenomenon.

Racism and Black Mental Health

After decades of research, Cross (1991, 1995) eventually revised the final stage of his nigrescence model, realizing that a positive racial identity does not necessarily equate to optimal psychological functioning (Vandiver et al., 2001). Early in the model's development, it was believed that resolution of anti-Black attitudes and the subsequent "self-love" that follows would also prevent various mental health issues among African Americans. However, as the model was tested and validated, Cross and his colleagues discovered that a positive racial identity does not always protect against mental health concerns or personality flaws (Vandiver et al., 2001). In fact, regardless of their level of racial identity development, many African Americans struggle with their mental health, and the numbers of African Americans with these struggles are on the rise. For example, according to data obtained from the Substance Abuse and Mental Health Services Administration (2020), the incidence of serious mental illness among African American adults increased from 2.5 percent in 2008 to 4.0 percent in 2019. Similarly, serious thoughts of suicide among this population also increased slightly between 2008 and 2019 from 3.6 percent to 4.0 percent.

Two mental health disorders that are seeing a particular increase in prevalence in the Black community are depression and anxiety. *The Washington Post* reports that at the beginning of 2020, approximately 36 percent of African Americans reported having struggles with both of these disorders (Fowers & Wan, 2020). While factors leading to depression and anxiety vary from genetic to environmental, research indicates that racism is a significant source of this psychological distress among African Americans. Additional statistics also reported in *The Washington Post*, for example, indicate that in the two days following the release of the video of George Floyd's death, rates of depression and anxiety among African Americans rose from 36 percent to 41 percent (Fowers & Wan, 2020). These findings illustrate how racism, even when experienced indirectly, can lead to a worsening of mood and affect. The findings are also consistent with other research which suggests that racism can have a broad impact on a variety of mental health concerns among African Americans including trauma (Carter, 2007), skin color satisfaction (Maxwell et al., 2015), self-esteem (Parham & Helms, 1985), career aspirations (Brown & Segrist, 2016), and overall life satisfaction (Pieterse et al., 2012).

Recognizing the impact of racism on one's mental health can be difficult for a variety of reasons. According to racialized trauma expert, Robert T. Carter (2007), one difficulty in understanding the relationship between racism and mental health is the fact that many individuals have never been made aware of the emotional and psychological toll racism has on its targets. Research conducted by Carter and Forsyth (2010) found that emotionally, reactions to racism most often include feeling disrespected, angry, insulted, disappointed, frustrated, outraged, hurt, or shocked. Other emotional reactions that were found to occur as a result of racism in their study, albeit to a lesser extent, included feeling irritated, annoyed, sad, rejected, demoralized, humiliated, inferior, helpless, confused or embarrassed, challenged, isolated, betrayed, and nervous. Psychologically, the researchers also found that racism leads to increased anxiety, hypervigilance, avoidance/numbing, and guilt/shame (Carter & Forsyth, 2010). This means that because of racism, many people of color lead lives full of worry, have a constant sense of being "on guard," suppress or deny their feelings about racism, and/or feel conflicted about not speaking out against racism. You can imagine, and perhaps know firsthand, that dealing with these thoughts and feelings repeatedly and over a prolonged period of time can eventually result in long-term worsening of one's mood, self-concept, relationships with others, and even one's physical health.

Another difficulty some Black people have in recognizing the impact of racism on their mental health has to do with general attitudes and cultural norms around mental health in the Black community. For example, many Black women are negatively affected by the strong Black woman myth (Abrams et al., 2014). This myth depicts Black women as having an unending well of strength, responsibility, and self-sacrifice. Accordingly, many Black women suffer with mental health struggles in silence, due to external and self-imposed pressure to suppress fear and weakness, resist being vulnerable or dependent, and succeed despite limited resources (Abrams et al., 2014, pp. 503–504). When thinking about racism and mental health, this means that while Black women may feel comfortable speaking out against the immorality or injustice surrounding racism, they may feel less comfortable acknowledging the emotional and psychological toll this form of oppression has on their lives and sense of self. Similarly, many Black men are also subjected to gendered racial norms that make it difficult for them to express the feelings of hurt, shame, and alienation often associated with racism (Payne, 2012). As a result, these men may also deny or fail to admit psychiatric symptoms, including those due to racism.

Finally, as we end this section, we'd like to make a few comments about the general nature of racism. There are many debates around the nature of racism, including who can be racist and whether or not racism still exists. In settling these debates, at least for the purpose of this book, it is important to note differences between racism and other related terms such as prejudice and discrimination. *Racial prejudice* refers to negative thoughts and feelings about an individual due to negative race-based stereotypes (DiAngelo, 2018), while *racial discrimination* can be defined as unequal treatment based on race (Pieterse et al., 2012). Examples of racial prejudice include beliefs that Black people are inferior, particularly when compared to White people, in terms of intelligence and morality. Examples of racial discrimination include being denied access to various career or social opportunities, being refused service in retail stores or restaurants, having one's qualifications questioned, or being treated as if you don't belong (Carter & Forsyth, 2010). *Racism* refers to the transformation of racial prejudice into systems of oppression through the use of power directed against members of racially marginalized racial groups (Carter, 2007). Essentially, the systemic nature of racism is what differentiates this construct from other similar terms, as racism is backed by the legal authority and institutional control of those at the top of the racial hierarchy, while prejudice and discrimination can be committed by any member of any racial group (DiAngelo, 2018). Moreover, it is the cumulative, ever-present quality of racism that is caused by its systemic nature that makes it so detrimental to the mental health of people of color.

Black is Beautiful and Black Lives Matter

Since European expansion into the New World, Black people have been demonized and portrayed as undesirable. As stated earlier, the original intent of this demonization was to legitimize the conquest and sale of African people; however, another consequence of this negative portrayal of Black people was an eroding of Black consciousness itself, leading to self-hatred and a psyche that in many ways also perceived White beauty as superior. The Black is Beautiful movement began in the 1960s with the goals of counteracting the harmful psychological impacts of negative messages about Black beauty and culture. This movement, as described by journalist Lilly Workneh (2022), initially started behind the camera of Kwame Brathwaite, a Harlem photographer who sought to overthrow the conventional Black aesthetic at the time, which favored White hair textures and styles, in favor of natural hair and African designs. Starting with a show titled "Naturally '62: The Original African Coiffure and Fashion Extravaganza Designed to Restore Our Racial Pride and Standards," Brathwaite's art quickly became popular and eventually led to a nation-wide phenomenon that not only embraced the physical beauty of people of African descent, but their cultural and intellectual strengths as well.

While there have been several decades since the 1960s, the spirit of the Black is Beautiful movement carries on today, as African Americans continue to live amid a social milieu (e.g., police brutality, racial profiling, and discrimination) that threatens our sense of identity, self-worth, and in some cases, our lives. In 2020, these threats reached a boiling point with the police killing of George Floyd, leading to worldwide recognition of another, burgeoning pro-Black movement known as Black Lives Matter (BLM). The BLM movement initially started in 2013 in response to the murder of Trayvon Martin, a 17-year-old African American boy who was killed by a neighbor while walking home from a convenience store. Christopher J. Lebron, author of *The Making of Black Lives Matter: A Brief History of an Idea*, tells Trayvon's story like this:

> The evening of February 26, 2012, Martin was walking through a Sanford, Florida community wearing a hoodie and holding only a soft drink and some candy. George Zimmerman, a neighborhood watch volunteer, deemed Martin suspicious and called the police though Martin had not actually done anything actionable—his only possible crime seemed to be walking while black. Though advised by the 911 operator to stand down and keep his distance, Zimmerman initiated a confrontation that resulted in a scuffle that ended with him shooting seventeen-year-old Martin dead. Despite Martin's younger age, weight, and size disadvantage, and the all-important fact that he was unarmed, his character quickly became the center of speculation and conversation—he was a black teenager wearing a hoodie, walking through someone else's neighborhood; if Zimmerman suspected him, he must have been suspect-worthy. It came as a surprise to some in America when, in the summer of 2013, Zimmerman was found not guilty on all charges related to Martin's death.
>
> (Lebron, 2017, p. ix)

Most of us remember the collective pain the Black community felt upon learning that another young African American man had been senselessly murdered ultimately due to racism, and the outrage we experienced upon his killer's acquittal. Needing some way to hold the system responsible, Alicia Garza, Patrisse Cullors, and Opal Tometi started #BlackLivesMatter as a call to action and a catalyst for change in the system that continually holds Black and White citizens to differing standards of accountability. Today, that call to action has evolved into a global phenomenon, with reach in the United States, the United Kingdom, and Canada. According to its website, BLM's mission is to "eradicate White supremacy and build local power to intervene in violence inflicted on Black communities by the state and vigilantes." While the organization has an official platform, it also maintains its grassroots quality, with local chapters that focus on issues affecting Black people in their communities.

In this book, we draw from the spirit of BLM and Black is Beautiful to help you embrace your racial identity and heal from the effects of racism. Our specific intention in honoring the spirit of both of these movements is to aid individuals in rewriting the anti-Black messages that say Black is not beautiful, while also promoting practices that contribute to joy and liberation among Black people. We know that this type of healing is not possible through just one book, yet we hope that it offers you a place to begin on your own journey to wellness.

Overview of the Remainder of this Workbook

The remainder of this workbook is organized into five parts: (1) Tools to Promote Healing from Racial Trauma, (2) Tools to Promote Self-Esteem, (3) Tools to Promote Resilience, (4) Tools to Promote Empowerment, and (5) Tools to Promote Community. Each part contains activities designed to help you heal from the negative psychological effects of racism and develop a more positive view of yourself as a Black person. Specifically, in Part 1: Tools to Promote Healing from Racial Trauma, we define key terms associated with racialized trauma and discuss strategies to mend the wounds of this outgrowth of racial oppression. Accordingly, activities in this part focus on: (a) examining your experiences with racism, (b) exploring your unique experience of racialized trauma, (c) identifying your personal psychological and emotional triggers, and (d) increasing your toolbox of strategies for coping and healing. In Part 2: Tools to Promote Self-Esteem, we continue our focus on individual healing, emphasizing ways to affirm your personal strengths, increase positive self-talk, and grow in racial and ethnic pride.

Parts 3, 4, and 5 of this workbook extend strategies for racial healing beyond the individual by exploring ways collective family and community supports may also be called upon to further enhance your ability to process and free yourself from any pain you might have around race. Part 3: Tools to Promote Resilience serves as a bridge between the individual and the collective by examining internal and external factors that help Black people develop the resilience needed to cope with adversities in life. Accordingly, activities in this part of the book explore ways you can use your personal strength, as well as your family, faith, and ancestor background, to bounce back from obstacles you might face. In Part 4: Tools to Promote Empowerment, we continue looking at ways you can gain confidence in your ability to assert control over your life. Therefore, activities in this part focus on factors that facilitate this sense of control, which is also known as empowerment, including consciousness, self-determination, leadership development, goal setting, sociopolitical engagement, and self-efficacy. You will also learn anti-racist strategies to disarm and challenge racial bias and discrimination. Lastly, we know that in the Black community, seeking help can be difficult due to a variety of factors that range from cultural norms against airing one's "dirty laundry" to fear of appearing weak in front of others. Therefore, activities in the final section of the book, Part 5: Tools to Promote Community, explore how to ask for help and seek support when needed, as well as the importance of being trustworthy and giving back to the community. Sacred people and places that traditionally offer safety and community are highlighted, and the part is concluded with activities to help you do some final reflections on who you are and your place in the Black community.

PART 1

Tools to Promote Healing from Racial Trauma

DOI: 10.4324/9781003221357-2

Close your eyes. Think back to your childhood and try to remember a time when you fell and scraped your knee while riding your bike. The first time you experienced this injury you may have been frightened and the pain may have felt intense, depending on your tolerance and the severity of your wound. Yet, with time, and perhaps a kiss and a Band-aid, you were probably able to recover from your injury without much lasting harm to your physical or emotional health.

Now, close your eyes again. Imagine if you fell and scraped your knee while riding your bike every day. Falling on a knee that was already tender because it hadn't had time to heal would probably intensify the pain you felt with each new injury. You might be worried and anxious while riding your bike, and you might even feel sad as you (a) blame yourself for not being a better bike rider or (b) believe that you are powerless to stop yourself from falling. When your physical wounds do finally heal, they may be thick and scarred and you may even have unseen internal damages to the bones and cartilage in your knee that affect you well into adulthood.

Just as falling off your bike may leave scars on your knees, negative experiences with race may also leave scars on your soul and wounds to your physical and emotional wellbeing. These scars, known as *racialized trauma*, occur as a result of repeated encounters with racism, prejudice, and discrimination, and lead to symptoms similar to those experienced with other forms of trauma and adversity. In the introduction to this part of the workbook, we define racialized trauma and discuss its emotional and physical effects. The activities that follow are designed to help you heal from racialized trauma as you explore its presence and impact in your life. During these activities, we will guide you in acknowledging the hurt, shame, and dehumanization associated with racialized trauma, and teach you skills to heal from the negative messages and experiences that lead to it. It is our hope that at the conclusion of this part, you will have gained insights that enable you to break free from the pain of racialized trauma as you travel on a path toward continued transformation and wellness.

What is Racialized Trauma?

Racialized trauma refers to mental and emotional injury caused by repeated encounters with racial bias, hostility, discrimination, or harassment (Carter, 2007). Common ways people are exposed to racialized trauma include small, everyday slights such as a store owner following a person of color around the store, racial slurs, denied opportunities, racial profiling, and hate crimes. These encounters, known as *race-based events*, may occur directly between individuals or groups of people, or they may happen indirectly, for example, as a result of watching a video of police brutality (Carter et al., 2020).

Whether they occur directly or indirectly, race-based events have a negative psychological effect on people of color and leave them feeling wounded. In your own experience, you may have noticed that even when you try to forget, forgive, or extend grace to perpetrators of race-based events, you are nonetheless left with the psychological mark of hurt that was caused by the act. While you may eventually be able to move forward, each new instance of discrimination, racism, or bias leads to additional wounds to your wellbeing. After repeated experiences you may start to question your self-worth and value, wondering, "What's wrong with me?" and "Why am I being treated like this?" You may additionally experience emotional reactions such as feelings of hopelessness, anger, shame, humiliation, and outright frustration, as well as behavioral reactions such as avoidance of situations in which you anticipate being the target of race-based events. Because racialized trauma is a result of accumulated effects over time, you may not even be aware that your reactions are in response to your encounters with race.

Racialized trauma has a real and lasting impact on how individuals see themselves, others, and the world. We are raised in a society that constantly floods us with negative messages and stereotypes about Black people, our culture, and even our bodies. These messages come from all around us—the television shows that depict Black people as unintelligent, criminal, prone to violence, and sexually promiscuous; the underrepresentation of Black people in positions of leadership and power; the overrepresentation of Black people in poverty, crime, and poor health statistics; and the lack of justice received by Black people in our judicial systems in the wake of events such as the killings of Breonna Taylor and George Floyd. Because of this flood of negative messaging, it is difficult to be Black and escape being affected by racialized trauma to some extent throughout the course of your life.

Like other forms of trauma, racialized trauma leads not only to mental and emotional distress, but also to changes in your brain and body. Keep reading to learn more about how racialized trauma is similar to other disorders such

Think About It

Read the following list of common reactions to racialized trauma. As you reflect on your own experiences with racial discrimination, what reactions have you seen within yourself?

- ❏ Worry
- ❏ Sadness
- ❏ Fear
- ❏ Anger
- ❏ Low self-esteem
- ❏ Poor concentration
- ❏ Frequent thoughts or memories about the event
- ❏ Avoiding people, places, or situations that remind you of the event

as posttraumatic stress disorder, including the emotional, behavioral, and physiological features that characterize trauma. As you read, reflect on your own experiences with race and think about how the characteristics of trauma may be evident in your own life.

Trauma and Triggers

Trauma is defined as an emotional response to a catastrophic or frightening event (American Psychiatric Association, 2013). Examples of these responses include anxiety, panic, shock, guilt, shame, hopelessness, sadness, and anger. Individuals with trauma fear for their safety and often become hypervigilant, or "on guard" for new or repeated threats to their safety. These individuals may also withdraw from their friends and family, have difficulty trusting others, and experience distressing symptoms such as nightmares, flashbacks, and intrusive thoughts. A woman subjected to intimate partner violence, for example, might feel shame about her situation, causing her to withdraw from her family and friends. She might also have nightmares about the abuse she has suffered, leading to difficulty sleeping, irritability, and poor concentration. If she were somehow able to escape her situation, she might nevertheless continue to have upsetting memories and nightmares, be easily startled, avoid people and places that remind her of the abuse, and continue to fear for her safety.

In a similar way, people who are discriminated against or harassed because of their race may also experience trauma due to fears for their safety. These individuals may avoid certain places to reduce the possibility of being physically or verbally attacked. To further protect themselves from harm, they might also make other adjustments such as changing the way they dress, distancing themselves from other Black people, or giving up various interests or hobbies (Nadal, 2018). These experiences are likewise associated with symptoms such as anxiety, depression, nightmares, hypervigilance, and physical complaints.

One unique aspect of trauma among Black people is that as a result of our prolonged exposure to racial oppression (for example, slavery, colonization, Apartheid, and segregation) we have also been subjected to historical, transgenerational, and vicarious trauma. *Historical trauma* refers to psychological distress that has been experienced by a group of people over time and across generations (Mohatt et al., 2014). An example would be the collective pain we felt with the murders of Trayvon Martin and Tamir Rice in light of the historical murders of Emmett Till and countless other young Black boys and girls. *Transgenerational trauma* is similar to historical trauma; however, this type of trauma refers to pain transmitted across generations due to events that occur within an individual family, for example, having a parent or a grandparent who was a victim of police brutality (Bryant-Davis et al., 2017).

Grieving for Those We've Lost

Over the past few years, we've been inundated with social media and news reports of police brutality resulting in the deaths of unarmed Black men, women, and children.

How do you feel when you learn about these deaths?

What resources can you draw on to heal from the pain caused by these losses? Some examples include:

- ❏ Religion and spirituality
- ❏ Community support
- ❏ Meditation
- ❏ Exercise
- ❏ Taking a break from social media and the news

Vicarious trauma, on the other hand, occurs as a result of learning about or witnessing racism or prejudice targeted at other Black people, for example, witnessing other Black people being bullied and called racial slurs (Nadal, 2018).

As you think about healing from racialized trauma, it is important to remember that trauma causes us to have certain emotions and do certain things, but trauma also lives within our bodies. This feeling of trauma in the body has been described as a physical sensation or surge of energy flowing from our brains and felt in the heart, lungs, and stomach (Menakem, 2017). Every so often, these feelings can be triggered when we find ourselves in situations that mimic the original trauma, such as in the presence of similar events, places, or perhaps certain people. These reminders are called *triggers.* Common triggers for racialized trauma are news and social media reports of race-based assaults or murders. Other triggers are specific to an individual's unique experiences and memories and may include details such as sights, sounds, smells, tastes, anniversaries, and thoughts that remind you of the trauma. While our body is designed to manage stress, too much prolonged stress and repeated exposure can become toxic for the body. In the next section, you will find information about the impact of racialized trauma on the brain. Later you'll have the opportunity to engage in mindfulness and relaxation activities to help regulate your brain's response to trauma.

Impact of Racialized Trauma on the Brain

The impact of racialized trauma on the brain is not seen with the naked eye. Behind the scenes, the three parts of the brain that respond to trauma—the amygdala, hippocampus, and prefrontal cortex—are working overtime to manage the hurt experienced with trauma. In fact, research shows that when you experience prolonged stress and trauma the brain produces more cortisol and norepinephrine. Cortisol affects the strength of the memories associated with traumatic events, and norepinephrine increases heart rate and controls the fight-or-flight response. These chemicals affect the processes that go on in the amygdala, hippocampus, and prefrontal cortex. The amygdala determines if a threat is present and sends out a signal to start the fight-or-flight response. When trauma has occurred, the amygdala remains hypervigilant even in the absence of a threat. The hippocampus, which is in charge of memories, also interacts with the amygdala by producing fragmented memories and flashbacks that trigger the amygdala's fight-or-flight response. The prefrontal cortex, which is the part of the brain responsible for emotion and behavior regulation, is less active in individuals who have experienced trauma and therefore less able to override the hippocampus and amygdala's fear response (Wolkin, 2016).

As you can see in the diagram, the behaviors and emotions experienced as a result of trauma are not only caused by your thought processes, but also by the activity that occurs in your brain. However, the brain does hold within it the power to heal and cope. Mindfulness can help interrupt the brain's cycle of negative thinking (Wolkin, 2016). Breathing exercises, for example, can help you to be present in the here and now rather than focused on the future. They also reduce stress by making your body feel more like it does when it's already relaxed. Other mindfulness strategies that focus on non-judgmental awareness and emotional regulation can also help you focus on the present moment by providing a space for you to observe and let go of your negative thinking.

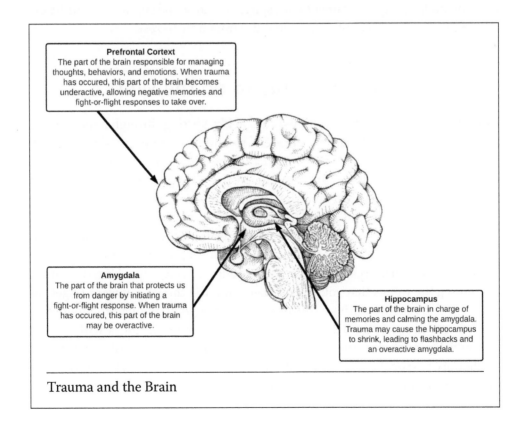

Prefrontal Cortext
The part of the brain responsible for managing thoughts, behaviors, and emotions. When trauma has occured, this part of the brain becomes underactive, allowing negative memories and fight-or-flight responses to take over.

Amygdala
The part of the brain that protects us from danger by initiating a fight-or-flight response. When trauma has occured, this part of the brain may be overactive.

Hippocampus
The part of the brain in charge of memories and calming the amygdala. Trauma may cause the hippocampus to shrink, leading to flashbacks and an overactive amygdala.

Trauma and the Brain

What Does it Take to Heal from Racialized Trauma?

Healing from racialized trauma is possible. Yet, with the current incidents of social injustice, police brutality, and reminders that you don't matter, combined with centuries of misdeeds leading to violence, poverty, mass incarceration, fragmented families, and health disparities in the Black community, it can be difficult to maintain hope. Nevertheless, know that by learning new ways of thinking and coping it is possible to find hope and overcome the wounds of racialized trauma. A first step is to look inwardly and remove the defenses covering up your trauma. When we experience a physical wound, we may wear a bandage or perhaps wear clothing so that the wound is not visible to others. Similar to someone who has experienced a physical injury to the body, you may have tried to cover up or hide the hurt of racialized trauma to make it less visible or less detectable. These coverups often take the form of overcompensating, suppressing feelings, and isolating yourself from the source of the hurt. After acknowledging the pain, shame, and negative ways of coping with racialized trauma, next steps include processing your feelings and learning how to cope using positive strategies such as journaling, mindfulness, and physical activity; finding ways to connect with spiritual and social supports; countering the dehumanizing effect of racism; and learning how to rest.

So, are you Ready to do the Work?

Completing the activities that follow can be like sorting through a mess in the closet. The items in the closet represent the memories and experiences you have from racialized trauma. Examples of these experiences might include being the target of a racial slur; wounds to your feelings of self-worth; limited access to finance, employment, education, healthcare, and housing; environmental racism such as the Flint, Michigan water crisis; or witnessing violent events and assaults. Every time you experience a new insult or trauma you fold it or throw it into the closet and eventually the closet is packed tight with all the memories and hurt. Treating the trauma entails slowing unpacking the closet, examining the things that you want to keep and the things you want to get rid of. You can begin or continue this process now as you complete the following worksheets designed to help you (a) examine your experiences with racism and racialized trauma, (b) explore the psychological impact of this trauma, (c) identify personal triggers, and (d) increase your repertoire of cognitive and behavioral strategies for coping and healing.

Racialized Trauma Self-Assessment Checklist

This self-assessment is designed to help you begin to explore your experience of racialized trauma. Read the statements in Table 1.1 and place a check mark under Yes or No, as the statement applies to you. Reflect on the qualities of racialized trauma you endorse as you complete the activities in this section.

TABLE 1.1

Racialized Trauma Self-Assessment Checklist

Question	Yes	No
1. I have been physically assaulted because of my race.		
2. I have been verbally assaulted because of my race.		
3. I have been denied access to resources such as loans, mentorship opportunities, promotions, etc. because of my race.		
4. I have been racially profiled by the police, store security, etc.		
5. I feel panic when I see the police.		
6. My work environment is hostile due to race-related issues.		
7. I have been mistreated on the basis of stereotypes.		
8. I have seen Black or other people of color mistreated because of their race.		
9. I feel guarded when around White people.		
10. I avoid being around Whites for fear of how the interaction might go.		
11. I feel sad about things connected to race/racism.		
12. I feel anxious or worried when around White people.		
13. I sometimes re-live negative encounters with race (e.g., have nightmares or daydreams about the event, ruminate about what happened)		
14. I experience a negative mood connected to race-based issues (e.g., anger, anxiety, or depression).		
15. I have physical complaints when I think about my experiences with race (e.g., stomachaches, muscle pain, rapid heart rate, difficulty breathing).		
16. I have negative thoughts about White people.		
17. I feel inferior when I compare myself to White people.		
18. I feel hopeless about the future at times because of race.		

Uncovering Your Racialized Trauma

Racialized trauma can create deep and lasting wounds. Treating these wounds can be painful, requiring lots of time, care, and support. Because these wounds are so deep, many individuals prefer to avoid dealing with this pain, focusing instead on protecting themselves from feeling the hurt caused by negative encounters with race. In fact, rather than dealing with their feelings directly, research shows that many people respond to race-related stress passively, for example, by isolating themselves from others or becoming emotionally numb (Polanco-Roman et al., 2016). While these strategies may offer some relief in the short-term, passive coping strategies often lead to other symptoms characteristic of traumatic stress including depression, anxiety, guilt, hypervigilance, and dissociation. So, while it may be natural, avoiding or denying the pain of racialized trauma can actually have a negative effect in the long run, worsening your mood and causing you to feel even more isolated and alone.

Use of active coping strategies, on the other hand, can help you manage the emotional and psychological pain that occurs as a result of racism and prejudice. Some of these strategies include becoming more racially conscious, taking action against racism on a systemic level, directly confronting perpetrators of racist events, seeking support from family and friends, and learning how to regulate your emotions (Forsyth & Carter, 2014). These strategies are discussed throughout this book. A first step, however, is simply acknowledging and creating space to deal with the emotional pain you've experienced. The following questions are designed to help you take this step. As you read these questions, please keep in mind that the goal of exploring racialized trauma is not to excuse or minimize the responsibility of racist individuals or systems, but rather to increase your awareness of how you've experienced the pain of this trauma. Doing so will allow you to more intentionally engage practices that will promote healing for your mind, body, and soul.

Recall three of your most memorable experiences with racism or prejudice. Write about them here. Include as many details as possible.

_____

_____

_____

_____

_____

_____

_____

_____

_____

_____

_____

_____

_____

_____

_____

Reflection Questions

1. What emotions did you feel during these experiences?

   _____

   _____

   _____

2. What emotions do you feel now as you remember these experiences?

   _____

   _____

   _____

3. What feelings do you notice in your body as you think about these experiences?

   _____

   _____

   _____

4. What changes in your behavior happened as a result of these experiences?

   _____

   _____

   _____

5. How have these situations changed the way you see yourself, others, and the world?

   _____

   _____

   _____

Sometimes it can be difficult to express the pain felt with racialized trauma. At other times, you may minimize the pain you feel, considering yourself "lucky" because you didn't wind up dead, in jail, or in the hospital like so many others. Yet, when thinking about racialized trauma, it is important to remember that this trauma occurs as a result of accumulated experiences with racism over time. Even the "little things" add up after a while.

In what follows, you will find three stories of individuals also dealing with the stress of race-based events in their everyday lives. As you read these stories, consider if there are experiences with racism and prejudice you may be overlooking. While these experiences may not have the same memorable impact as the events you described earlier, they nonetheless may have a significant effect on your mood and how you think about yourself.

Meet Joshua

Joshua is a 30-year-old African American man who recently lost his job as a plant supervisor due to low ratings on back-to-back performance evaluations. Since that time, Joshua has experienced an overwhelming sense of anger and frustration and has made little effort to find new employment. Joshua was the only African American person in a position of leadership at the plant. Initially, he believed he would do well as a plant supervisor; however, he started worrying and second guessing himself shortly after getting the job. Some of Joshua's anxiety was caused by his awareness that he was held to a higher standard of performance than his peers. Other supervisors at the plant did the bare minimum and were never criticized, but Joshua had to go above and beyond to prove his worth. Now that he has lost his job, Joshua has become unsure about his ability to be a supervisor and has started to wonder if he should stick to working on the assembly line. This idea also causes Joshua to worry, as his family can't survive on a lower paying job.

1. What other feelings do you think Joshua may have experienced besides anger, frustration, and worry?

_____

_____

_____

2. How does Joshua's experience compare to situations you've experienced in your own life?

    _____

    _____

    _____

Meet Imani

Imani is a 21-year-old woman who immigrated to the United States from Jamaica in order to attend college. Having grown up in a majority Black country, Imani was initially shocked by the frequent encounters with racism she experienced when she first arrived at her predominantly White university. During her freshman year, Imani felt isolated from most of the students in her dorm, as she was rarely invited to social gatherings or study groups. A few times she even overheard students mock her accent and question her right to be in the country. Imani confronted the students on these occasions but was labeled as hostile and angry as a result. Eventually, Imani was able to connect with other Black students on campus, which helped to decrease her sense of isolation to some extent. However, with graduation approaching, Imani finds herself facing a new set of challenges as she notices a lack of interest from prospective employers at career fairs in spite of her excellent academic record and experience. Imani has also noticed the way some White students in her program seem to have help finding jobs from professors, causing her to feel rage about the lack of fairness in how students are helped to be successful in her program.

1. How did you feel emotionally as you read Imani's story? What feelings did you notice in your body?

    _____

    _____

    _____

2. Imani felt rage about the lack of fairness in her academic program. How do you feel when things are unfair based on race?

    _____

    _____

    _____

Meet Cynthia

Cynthia is a 40-year-old African American woman who recently earned a highly coveted CEO position at her company. Cynthia has worked hard to be successful in corporate life, sacrificing time with her family as well as her own self-care needs. In spite of her hard work, Cynthia is frequently insulted by seemingly neutral comments and events in the workplace such as being mistaken for the administrative assistant by visitors or being complimented for how articulate she is. When she goes home at night, Cynthia feels upset by what she experiences at work; however, she also feels just as upset with herself for not confronting her colleagues about their behavior. Cynthia has started to lose sleep over the issue and is tired of having to prove herself at work. She feels sad and confused because what she thought would be her dream job has actually turned out to be a source of disappointment and stress.

1. What has been your experience with "small" instances of racism or prejudice?

   _____

   _____

   _____

2. How do you handle these instances?

   _____

   _____

   _____

You can see from the stories of Joshua, Imani, and Cynthia that events leading to racialized trauma happen across a variety of settings and in a variety of ways. As you continue with the activities in this part of the workbook, we want to encourage you not to minimize any of the experiences you've had with racism and prejudice in your life. None of these experiences are too small to matter. What matters is how they make you feel and the meaning they have for you.

Before moving on to the next activity, we recommend that you take a break. Dealing with painful memories can be overwhelming and exhausting. Give yourself space to release any negative energy that may have built up while exploring these memories by doing something you find nurturing such as listening to some encouraging music or going for a walk.

Identifying Internalized Racism

One important part of racial healing is dealing with internalized racism. *Internalized racism* is a negative view of yourself based on the perceived inferiority of your own racial background (Steele & Newton, 2022). People develop internalized racism when they accept negative racial stereotypes about themselves and believe in the superiority of the beauty, language, norms, and traditions of other racial groups, particularly those of White people (Bailey et al., 2014).

Internalized racism often leads to self-hatred and a low sense of self-worth, but it is different from similar concepts such as low self-esteem because internalized racism leads to ideas and behaviors that reinforce racial oppression (Bivens, 2005). People with internalized racism, for example, often feel so overwhelmed by their feelings of shame and alienation that they perceive themselves as powerless to initiate change in their environments, which allows racism to go unchallenged.

In the Introduction chapter of this workbook, we discussed several factors that may lead to internalized racism among Black people. Many of these factors are historical, such as the history of slavery and segregation in the United States. Others are ongoing, such as the negative images of Black people shown throughout the media, in addition to attitudes that minimize the impact of racism on a person's life or suggest Black people are to blame for difficulties that are actually caused by racism. Some of these attitudes are

Copyright material from Janeé M. Steele and Charmeka S. Newton (2023) *Black Lives Are Beautiful*, Routledge

37

Colorblind Racial Attitudes

Colorblind racial attitudes imply that racism is no longer an obstacle for people of color, which makes it difficult to challenge or even acknowledge racism in various settings (Tawa et al., 2016). The "All Lives Matter" social media campaign is one example of a colorblind racial attitude that has been particularly hurtful for Black people in light of the ongoing killings of unarmed Black people by the police and community vigilantes.

What other colorblind racial attitudes have you experienced?

What effect have these attitudes had on your relationships and how you see people in your various work, school, and social settings?

known as colorblind racial attitudes. *Colorblind racial attitudes* refer to the belief that race should not and does not matter (Neville et al., 2013). Examples of common statements that reflect colorblind racial attitudes are, "When I look at you, I don't see race" and "I don't have a racist bone in my body." While colorblind racial attitudes may seem harmless, they can cause people to doubt or question if racism is at play in their lives, further adding to the stress they experience. Colorblind racial attitudes, however, actually perpetuate racism by ignoring the roles race and racism have in people's lives, as well the privileges afforded to members of the White race.

Another type of belief that minimizes the impact of racism on the lives of Black people is called a *legitimizing myth*. Legitimizing myths refer to beliefs that are used to justify prejudice and inequality in our country. For example, during slavery, the legitimizing myth that Africans were ignorant, immoral, and without religion was used to validate the slave trade, painting enslavers as altruistic saviors rather than captors. After slavery was abolished, a new legitimizing myth was adopted, this time to justify segregation (Steele, 2020). Whereas Black people were previously viewed as meek and created by God to be in service to others, this legitimizing myth portrayed Black people as hostile and criminal, needing to be kept away from the White public at all costs. Today, both of these legitimizing myths remain evident with notions such as "the welfare queen," which paints a picture of Black women as lazy and taking advantage of the system, and the characterization of Black men as "thugs," which results in more frequent and harsher sentencing for Black people in our criminal justice system.

Colorblind racial attitudes and legitimizing myths are both grounded in White supremacy. *White supremacy* is a way of thinking that promotes Whiteness as the standard for all of humanity (DiAngelo, 2018). This includes standards for beauty, speech, and relating to other people. The ways in which White supremacy affects some aspects of culture is obvious, for example, preferences for lighter skin and eyes, straight hair, and use of standard English over African American English vernacular. Other aspects of White supremacy may not be as openly acknowledged, but are powerful, nonetheless. These aspects of White supremacy include the messages of superiority conveyed by the fact that White people lead in positions of power in nearly all aspects of society, including education, medicine, law, government, finance, and the military (DiAngelo, 2018). For example, a recent survey from the U.S. Department of Education found that approximately 80% of all public-school and 85% of all private-school teachers in the United States are White (Taie & Goldring, 2020). Having so few Black and other people of color in these roles is often taken for granted and gives credibility to the idea that White people are naturally superior, and that Black and other people of color are inferior by default.

Because White supremacy operates on so many levels, it becomes the lens through which we see the world, whether we want to or not. Seeing yourself and others outside of the lens of White supremacy requires you to take an intentional look at the ways in which you have internalized the messages of racism and White supremacy. Starting from childhood, we are inundated with messages from the media, our schools, and even our families that negatively influence how we see ourselves as Black people. Each time we are exposed to these messages, the idea that Black culture is inferior becomes more and more deeply ingrained in our minds on both conscious and subconscious levels. This sense of inferiority impacts how we interpret and respond to everyday situations, whether race is directly or indirectly involved. Consider the following two scenarios:

Kyra

Kyra is an attractive woman who was often told "You're pretty for a dark-skinned girl" by friends and family while growing up. Although meant as a compliment, Kyra interpreted this statement to mean that she would never be as pretty as a woman with lighter skin, a belief she initially developed during childhood. As an adult, this belief continues to be reinforced through cues from her environment, for example, by the dating preferences of the most desirable prospects in her dating pool and by the women who are considered most attractive in the entertainment industry. When faced with these cues, Kyra realizes the differences in skin color between herself and women who are considered most beautiful and she feels inferior when she compares herself to them. As a result, Kyra engages in behavior such as staying out of the sun to avoid becoming darker and developing a preference for partners with lighter skin, hoping that her children will be lighter and therefore more attractive, which not only continues the cycle of colorism among Black people, but also reinforces her feelings of self-hatred related to her skin color.

Jason

Jason is the hiring manager at a successful accounting firm. He volunteers at a local community center where he gives frequent talks to young men about job skills and how to be successful in the workforce. During his talks, Jason emphasizes the importance of fitting into corporate culture in terms of dress, speech, and personal grooming. Jason describes certain hairstyles such as braids and afros as "unprofessional" and encourages the men to opt for something that looks less "unkempt."

Jason is a successful man who is attempting to give back to the young men in his community by teaching them how to be successful in their own careers. While Jason's intentions may be good, the messages behind some of his advice regarding personal grooming actually reinforce racist ideas that certain hairstyles and textures natural to Black hair are somehow unprofessional or a source of shame. For many Black people, natural hair is an important source of their identity, representing pride in their cultural heritage or even a sense of freedom. By discouraging the young men in his group from wearing natural hairstyles, Jason is inadvertently perpetuating corporate standards that urge Black people to conform or assimilate their appearance into White norms. Jason could have chosen instead to be honest about the challenge the men may face in their work environments if they chose to wear their hair in certain ways and helped to prepare them with knowing what to do and say in these situations, emphasizing that the choice is theirs to make. In this example, the evidence of White supremacy is clear—White standards are viewed as the norm, and Black people are expected to adjust to these standards without question or opposition.

Recap

Here are some of the most important points we've covered regarding internalized racism:

1. Internalized racism happens when Black people accept negative stereotypes about their own racial group and believe, often on a subconscious level, in the superiority of White cultural norms and standards of beauty.
2. When people have internalized racism, they often experience a sense of shame and alienation about certain aspects of being Black, for example, dark skin, Black patterns of speech, Black sounding names, kinky hair, etc.

40

3. Internalized racism is different than low self-esteem because it results in thinking or behavior that reinforces racism. Believing that Black people are disproportionately represented in the criminal justice system because of moral failings in the Black community such as single parent households, or adjusting parts of how you look, speak, or act to fit into White cultural standards, for example, reinforces racism because these attitudes and behaviors (a) give credibility to the idea that Black people are inherently inferior and (b) continue the practice of White people setting the standard to which all other racial groups must strive to obtain.

Remember, internalized racism and the White supremacy that serves as its foundation often operates like an invisible pair of glasses through which we see the world. Because of this, you may not always be aware of the thoughts you have that reflect internalized racism. Instead, you may feel a twinge of embarrassment, shame, or even anger somewhere in your body when confronted with images and situations that seem to confirm negative Black stereotypes. With this and the aspects of internalized racism listed earlier in mind, think back to the negative stereotypes about Black people you identified in Part 1 of this workbook and fill in the details in Table 3.1, exploring ways in which internalized racism has affected your life. Thinking about any colorblind racial attitudes and legitimizing myths you have been introduced to in the past may help.

TABLE 3.1

Naming Internalized Racism in My Own Life

Naming Internalized Racism in My Own Life

Think back over your life and try to identify times in which you may have been affected by internalized racism. Perhaps you felt embarrassed about certain aspects of your identity that were associated with being Black, or maybe you felt angry toward other Black people for behaving in stereotypical ways. Explore these situations in this chart, identifying the stereotypes, negative thoughts, feelings, and behaviors associated with each situation. The first two rows are completed using information from the scenarios with Kyra and Jason.

Situation	Stereotype	Thoughts	Feelings	Behavior			
Thinking about my own physical attractiveness and what I want in a partner	People with lighter skin are more beautiful	Even though I am pretty, I am less beautiful than people with lighter skin	Sad, less than (inferior)	Avoid getting darker from the sun; seek a romantic partner with lighter skin			
Teaching Black youth how to be successful in the workplace	Black hairstyles and ways of being are unprofessional	In order to be successful, Black people must conform to White standards	Resigned to the fact that this is the way the world works, powerless to create change	Adjust personal looks and behavior to be similar to those of White colleagues			

42

Reflection Questions

1. After completing the table, what are the most common thoughts and feelings you have related to internalized racism?

   _____

   _____

   _____

   _____

   _____

2. How do these thoughts and feelings affect your behavior?

   _____

   _____

   _____

   _____

   _____

3. What are some alternative explanations for the stereotypes leading to your internalized racism?

   _____

   _____

   _____

   _____

   _____

4. What should you think or do differently?

   _____

   _____

   _____

   _____

   _____

Interrupting the Cycle of Internalized Racism

In Activity 3, you began exploring the cycle of internalized racism in your life. You saw from that exercise that one of the saddest manifestations of prolonged exposure to racism occurs when people of color begin to internalize racism by endorsing negative racial stereotypes and adopting White cultural standards as the norm. Beyond feelings of shame or humiliation, one of the reasons internalized racism can be so harmful is that it leads to support of the status quo by causing people of color to do things like:

❏ Alter their appearance or behavior to meet White cultural norms, which gives validity to the idea that White ways of being are superior
❏ Accommodate the needs and emotions of White people by avoiding racial discourse or anything that would be perceived as threatening to White people
❏ Feel helpless or powerless to change their situation, and therefore never try
❏ Look down on people from their own race
❏ Deny that racism even exists

Internalized racism is not a result of a character defect, weakness, ignorance, or shortcoming on your part (Pyke, 2010). Instead, internalized racism is a result of experiencing the frequent invalidation, minimization, and discrimination of White supremacy. You can understand internalized racism as a cycle

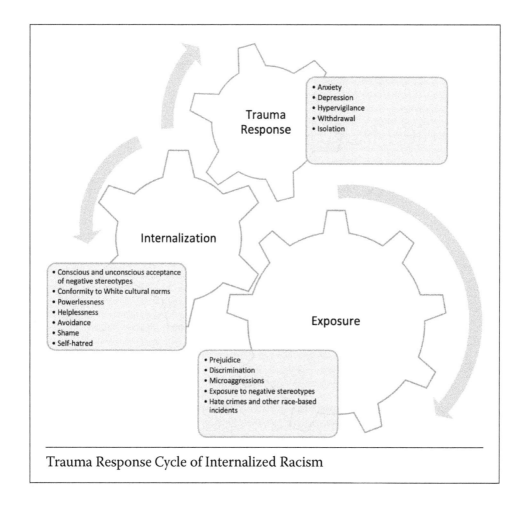

Trauma Response
- Anxiety
- Depression
- Hypervigilance
- Withdrawal
- Isolation

Internalization
- Conscious and unconscious acceptance of negative stereotypes
- Conformity to White cultural norms
- Powerlessness
- Helplessness
- Avoidance
- Shame
- Self-hatred

Exposure
- Prejuidice
- Discrimination
- Microaggressions
- Exposure to negative stereotypes
- Hate crimes and other race-based incidents

Trauma Response Cycle of Internalized Racism

of exposure that often results in a trauma response. In the Trauma Response Cycle shown here, you can see that through constant experiences with prejudice, discrimination, and negative images in the media, people of color develop conscious and unconscious acceptance of a racial hierarchy in which Whites are consistently deemed as superior to people of color. This leads to symptoms of trauma, which are reinforced and worsened through continued exposures.

Identifying new ways of thinking about yourself can help reduce the effects of internalized racism in your life. In Activity 3, you identified alternative explanations for negative stereotypes applied toward you and other Black people. With these alternatives in mind, let's work toward identifying something you would like to believe about yourself outside of these stereotypes. For example, if you struggle to accept your hair texture or the color of your skin, you might develop a statement such as, "My hair and my skin are beautiful. The way they are naturally allows me to enjoy things in life like swimming, running, or being out in the sun freely and without worry. I don't have to be inconvenienced or shamed into fitting into a certain standard of beauty."

> Random. Do you think things like weaves, perms, and colored contacts might be a form of internalized racism?

> To some extent. But it depends on the thinking behind it.

> Ok. I was asking because I have a presentation at work tomorrow and whenever I do professional presentations I always question if I should take my weave out if I have one in at the time. And whenever I teach, I wear my glasses. I can have contacts on all day long, but when it's time to teach I put my glasses on because I think it will make White students take me more seriously. And I can barely talk because I am so focused on not sounding too Black. I need therapy, lol

Sometimes coming up with new ways of thinking about yourself can be difficult. Have you ever noticed that coming up with solutions to your own problems can seem almost impossible, but you have plenty of good advice for friends? Externalizing your problems by pretending you're giving advice to a friend can actually be an effective strategy to challenge negative thinking in your own life. The dialogue exchange shown here is an actual text message that occurred between two African American friends. In the text message you will see one of the friends is expressing some of her internalized racism. Take a moment and read the text message. As you read the conversation, think about how you might respond to this person if they were your friend.

In this exchange, the one friend is being totally transparent with her friend about her struggles with internalized racism. It appears the friend is struggling with coming across as "too Black," which in her mind is connected with not being professional. The friend also appears to be struggling with "sounding Black," signaling that she may also have negative thoughts associated with African American dialects of speech.

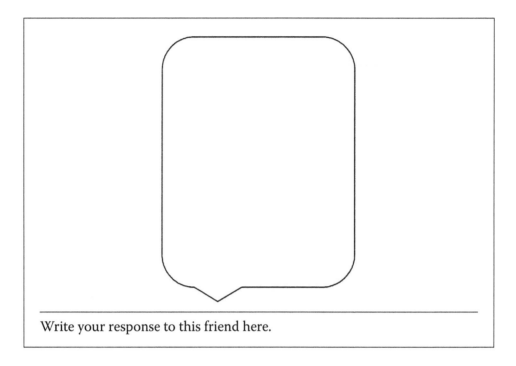

Write your response to this friend here.

In the blank text message bubble, send a text message back to the person that is affirming of their identity. You may even use what you learned earlier about internalized racism to help the person.

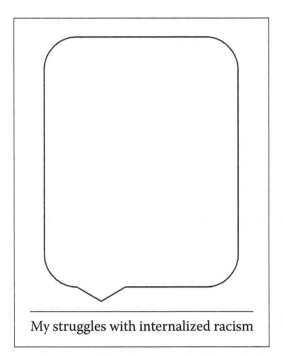

My struggles with internalized racism

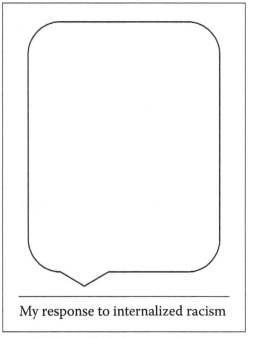

My response to internalized racism

Now, pretend you're sending a message to your best friend or someone who you can be totally transparent with and discuss ways in which you engage in internalized racism behaviors. In the first text bubble, write your message about your struggle with internalized racism. Next, send back a text message to yourself that is affirming and can be used to remind yourself of the false ideas leading to internalized racism. As you develop this message, think about any evidence in your life that refutes any negative stereotypes you may believe about yourself, as well as aspects of Black culture in which you sense strength, beauty, and support.

Reflection Questions

1. What messages have been most harmful to you having a positive racial identity?

_____

_____

_____

2. What new messages do you need to hear to replace the old, negative messages?

_____

_____

_____

3. Where or from whom can you get support in developing these new messages?

_____

_____

_____

Your Body Can Help

In this section of the workbook, you've learned that racialized trauma not only affects your emotions and how you think, but also the sensations you feel in your body. Some of these sensations include a racing heartbeat, muscle tension, stomachaches, headaches, and tiredness; however, the physical effects of trauma go beyond those you may be consciously aware of, such as the pit in your stomach or the ache in your chest, to include changes in the development of your brain (Wolkin, 2016). Specifically, neuroscience research shows that the three areas of the brain responsible for detecting and responding to threats undergo significant changes due to trauma. In the brain of a person who has experienced trauma, these three parts of the brain—the amygdala, hippocampus, and prefrontal cortex—are overstimulated in the areas in charge of memory and the fight, flight, or freeze response, and understimulated in the area in charge of telling the brain when to calm down. As a result, people who have experienced trauma may have flashbacks of traumatic events and be constantly on the lookout for danger.

Because there is such a strong connection between your body and trauma, your body can be one of the most powerful tools you have when coping with the pain of racialized trauma. In fact, trauma experts believe that since trauma lives in the parts of the brain that activate the body in the face of danger, thinking or talking about your trauma isn't enough to promote healing alone (Menakem, 2017). During a traumatic response, the parts of your brain responsible for emotions, memory, and survival (often referred to as the mammalian and reptilian brain) temporarily override the part of your brain responsible for regulating emotions and rational thinking (referred to as the human brain). When this occurs, the brain sends electric and chemical impulses throughout your body that become imprinted as physical sensations you can feel (Sweeton, 2017). For example, your heart may race, your breathing might become shallow, your muscles might become tense, or you may experience a surge of adrenaline. At the same time, your brain's implicit memory connects these sensations to details from the traumatic event such as a smell or a tone of voice. These details then become triggers that reinitiate the traumatic response felt in your body again and again.

With trauma, your brain becomes stuck in the pattern described earlier because you never receive the signal that danger is over or not present. You can often tell that a person's body is storing trauma just by looking at it. Think about your own body's response to trauma. Are your back and shoulders usually tense? Is your neck often stiff? Does your heart start to race at the slightest mention of racial divisions? If so, it may be beneficial for you to spend some time learning how to heal your body's response to trauma through techniques focused on movement and bringing awareness to your body. In what follows, you'll find several exercises to help you calm the chemical impulses telling you that you are in danger. If you are unfamiliar with these types of exercises, they may feel uncomfortable at first—that's ok. Addressing the trauma in your life can be overwhelming and frightening. Because of this, we recommend that you identify people who can support you through this process if you need it such as family, friends, a therapist, or church and community organizations. You may also find that you just don't like some of these activities. That's ok too. People respond to painful events in unique ways, and healing from this pain is also unique to each individual. What's important is that you find what works for you in terms of identifying and releasing the physical manifestations of trauma in your body.

Body Scan Meditation

In order to release the trauma stored up in your body, you must first increase your awareness of the physical symptoms your body experiences. One way to increase this awareness is through a body scan meditation. A body scan meditation involves noticing your bodily sensations in a gradual sequence from your feet to your head. Taking the time to scan yourself in this way helps you to get to know your body better and alerts you to any pain or discomfort you might be experiencing (Scott, 2020). Having this awareness allows you to be more intentional in implementing tools from your box of coping strategies when necessary for better psychological functioning in the long-term. To do a body scan, complete the following steps:

1. **Get in a comfortable position**. Many people are most comfortable doing a body scan while laying down. If laying down is uncomfortable or not possible for you, you can also sit in a chair. The most important thing is to have a relaxed and open body posture. You can also close your eyes if this feels comfortable for you.

2. **Take some deep breaths**. After getting in a comfortable position, allow yourself a few moments to take some deep breaths. You can use the diaphragmatic breathing method described on p. XX, or you can simply breathe in through your nose for four counts, hold your breath gently for two counts, and breathe out of your mouth as if you are blowing through a straw.

3. **Bring your attention to your feet**. Once you've taken some deep breaths, bring your attention to your feet, noticing any sensations you might feel. These sensations might include aches, pains, tingling, tension, shaking, heaviness, or pressure. As you notice these sensations, continue to breathe and observe the feelings without judgment or trying to stop the feeling.

4. **Scan the rest of your body**. When you're ready, gradually move from your feet up through the rest of your body, continuing to breathe and notice any sensations you might be experiencing. As you scan your body, it's likely that your attention may wander. This is normal. When this occurs, simply bring your attention back to scanning your body, again, without judgment or criticism. Continue this process until you've made it to the top of your head. Once you are finished, spend a few more minutes breathing and then move into the rest of your day either by implementing one of the other strategies in this section or by moving forward with any kind of goal-directed behavior.

Reflection Questions

1. As you completed your body scan, what sensations did you notice and where did you notice them?

    _____

    _____

    _____

    _____

    _____

    _____

    _____

2. What physical activities can you do to release some of the tension or pain you noticed in your body?

    _____

    _____

    _____

    _____

    _____

    _____

    _____

3. What goal-directed behavior can you engage in now? For example, what can you do to feel accomplished or to help someone else?

    _____

    _____

    _____

    _____

    _____

    _____

    _____

Use Your Senses

The five senses are important when dealing with trauma because the information we receive from our senses can affect how we feel. For example, for those who love Christmas, seeing Christmas lights, hearing Christmas music, or smelling the scent of a Christmas tree puts them in pleasant mood. With racialized trauma, experimenting with sensory inputs can help you to positively cope by soothing intense emotions. Touch and movement are especially effective in calming a hyper-aroused nervous system. Table 5.1 identifies a few activities you might use to calm your brain and regulate your emotions. Try some of the activities over the next few days to see how they affect your mood.

TABLE 5.1

Sensory Activities to Soothe Trauma

Sense	Activity
Taste	• Drink some hot tea or hot chocolate • Enjoy a healthy treat such as an apple or trail mix • Chew a piece of gum • Have a small piece of dark chocolate
Touch	• Take a hot shower or a bath • Ask for a hug • Get a massage • Give yourself a hand or a neck massage • Pet a soft animal • Go outside and feel the sun on your skin for a short while • Stand barefoot on the earth
Smell	• Light a scented candle • Use a diffuser with lavender or other essential oils • Wear a scented lotion or cologne
Sound	• Listen to an encouraging podcast • Listen to the sounds of nature in a recording or outdoors • Play calming or encouraging music • Sing your favorite song
Sight	• Introduce plants or flowers into your home or work environment • Use guided imagery to visualize yourself in a place that feels relaxing and refreshing • Do an affirming guided meditation and envision yourself strong and empowered • Look at a photograph of a loved one or cherished memory

Record the activities you like on the hand shown here and refer back to it whenever you are feeling stressed or overwhelmed by racial tensions in your life.

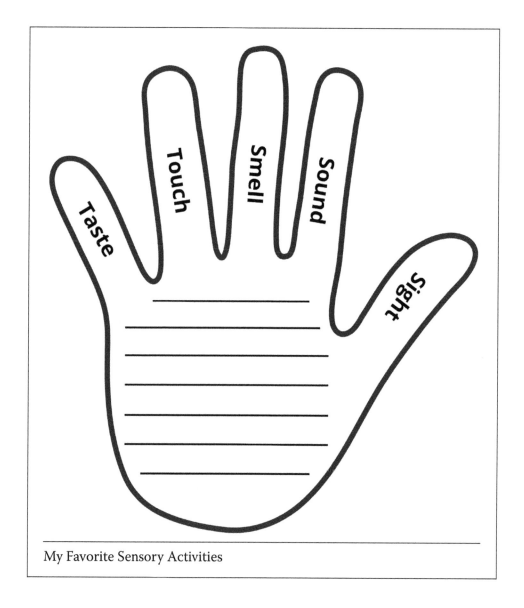

My Favorite Sensory Activities

Reflection Questions

1. In what three situations do you most frequently experience physical symptoms of trauma?

   _____

   _____

   _____

2. What would be the most effective sensory activities for you to use in each situation?

   _____

   _____

   _____

   _____

Ground Yourself with the Five Senses Mindfulness Technique

The Five Senses Mindfulness Techniques, also known as the 5-4-3-2-1 Method, is a popular grounding technique used to help individuals calm themselves, particularly during anxiety and panic attacks. *Grounding* is a term used to describe techniques that help you interrupt flashbacks, disturbing memories, and physiological responses such as rapid heartbeat and faster breathing by helping you to connect to and focus on the present moment. As we've previously discussed, racial trauma does often lead to PTSD-like symptoms such as anxiety and panic (Carter et al., 2020). A panic attack is a sudden and intense fear that triggers physical symptoms such as rapid heart rate, sweating, trembling, shortness of breath, hot flashes, chills, stomachaches, headaches, dizziness, chest pains, numbness, and dizziness or fainting. Through use of grounding, individuals are able to separate themselves from their distressing physical and emotional feelings and move through their pain. To try grounding with the Five Senses Mindfulness Technique, follow these five simple steps:

1. Identify **five** things you can see around you
2. Identify **four** things you can touch around you
3. Identify **three** things you can hear

4. Identify **two** things you can smell
5. Identify **one** thing you can taste

Reflection Questions

1. What has been your experience with anxiety and panic attacks?

   _____

   _____

   _____

2. What situations tend to trigger a panic response in you?

   _____

   _____

   _____

3. What other ways can you refocus on the here and now during a panic attack other than the 5-4-3-2-1 Method? Examples include taking a walk or identifying all of the details in something small in your environment such as a penny or a paperclip.

   _____

   _____

   _____

Take a Break and Breathe

Race-based events usually catch us off guard. You may be scrolling through social media or catching up on the news and suddenly be confronted with yet another instance or reminder of the social injustices faced by Black people in this country. Or you may be going about an everyday task such as running an errand to the bank or grocery store where you're undeservingly treated as if you were suspicious or don't belong. In these situations, it can be helpful to simply take a break and breathe. Breathing exercises are one of the most effective practices for trauma survivors because they help lower your heart rate and the effects of cortisol (Jewell & Hoshaw, 2021). In the introduction to this part of the workbook, we told you that individuals who have experienced trauma have an increased level of cortisol production, which strengthens the memory of traumatic events, leading to signals in the brain that activate the fight-or-flight response. Breathing exercises can help to interrupt this cycle by calming physiological signs such as a rapid heartbeat or faster breathing that are telling your brain you're in danger.

One of the more popular breathing exercises is called *diaphragmatic breathing* or *belly breaths.* The diaphragm, which is a large muscle located at the base of the lungs, assists breathing by giving you more power to empty your lungs. This helps you to relax and introduces more oxygen into your bloodstream. To practice diaphragmatic breathing, begin by laying on your back with your knees bent and head supported, or by sitting in a chair with your knees bent and your shoulders and neck in a relaxed position. Then, follow these steps:

1. Place one hand on the center of your chest and the other hand on your stomach just below your rib cage.
2. With your hands in place, breathe in, making the hand on your stomach push out as you do. This may feel awkward at first, as your natural reflex may be to suck your stomach in to draw your breath. Try to resist this urge, drawing your breath from your lungs instead. Practice this for a few breaths. Once you've got it, move on to step 3.
3. Keeping your hands on your chest and stomach, focus on your breath as you breathe out, moving your stomach inward as you exhale. Practice for a few breaths and then continue to step 4.
4. Once you've got the breathing technique down, still with your hands on your chest and stomach, breathe in for four counts, hold for one count, and then breathe out for six counts, nice and slow.
5. Continue this process for at least 20 breaths, stopping once you feel calm and your physiological responses begin to rest.

Relax

Much like breathing exercises, relaxation techniques can also interrupt the distressing physiological symptoms you experience in response to trauma. One relaxation technique, called progressive muscle relaxation, is a technique that allows you to relax your body when you've become tense.

In this progressive muscle relaxation exercise, you will tense each muscle for about 5 seconds and then relax the muscle for about 30 seconds. It may be helpful as you tense the muscle to count slowly in your head. If you have any pain or discomfort, it is ok to skip that muscle group. As you do this exercise, visualize your muscles tensing and then visualize warm energy flowing through you as you relax the muscle. Make sure that you use deep slow breathing throughout the exercise.

Now, Let's Begin

Get into a comfortable position. You may sit or lay down. Soothing, wordless music playing in the background may help the experience.

Begin by breathing air slowly into your nose and out through your mouth. You should feel your chest slowly rise and fall.

Take in another deep breath, hold it, and slowly release.

When you're ready, move your attention to your feet. Curl your toes inward so that your feet arch. Hold them for 5 seconds. Feel the tension and slowly release them as you count to 30.

Observe the new feeling of relaxation in your feet.

Next, tense the muscles of your legs. Squeeze your legs together and feel the tension in your legs and pelvic area. Hold the tension for 5 seconds and slowly relax your leg muscles as you count to 30. Feel your legs slowly fall separate from each another.

Observe the new feeling of relaxation in your legs and pelvis.

Now, move to your arms. Tense your hands as though you are making fists. Feel the tension in your hands and upper biceps. Count to 5 and then slowly release the tension of your hands and arms by releasing your fists slowly as you count to 30.

Observe the new feeling of relaxation in your arms.

Next, tense your shoulders, bringing your shoulders up to your ears for 5 seconds. Then, slowly release your shoulder muscles as you count to 30.

Observe the new feeling of relaxation in your shoulders.

Lastly, tense your face muscles, frowning and holding for 5 seconds. Then, slowly release your face muscle as you count to 30.

Observe the new feeling of relaxation in your face.

Now, scan your body for any tension. If your notice any remaining tension, work to relax that part of your body as you hold the muscle group for 5 seconds and then slowly relax for 30 seconds.

Before you leave this muscle relaxation exercise, return your focus to your breathing. Take some nice slow breaths in through your nose and breathe out through your mouth.

Congratulations! You just completed your first muscle relaxation exercise and your body thanks you!

Challenge: Over the next day or so think of a way you can incorporate breathing, muscle relaxation, or any of the other strategies discussed in this activity into your daily routine, as there is power in being intentional.

A Healing
Self-Compassion
Meditation

Knowing how to comfort yourself is essential when healing from racialized trauma. Self-compassion meditations offer a way of providing yourself with this comfort. Meditation has been found to have several positive effects for African Americans, including a reduction of blood pressure, heart rate, anxiety, depression, and self-criticism (Bell, 2015; Johnson et al., 2018). Moreover, meditation teaches us ways of thinking about ourselves that challenge the negative thoughts introduced into our minds through racism and racialized trauma. In particular, meditation teaches us to be non-judgmental, loving, kind, accepting, and compassionate toward ourselves. For people who have experienced racialized trauma, self-compassion can be especially beneficial. Racialized trauma causes significant pain and suffering. With racialized trauma you may experience feelings of helplessness, hopelessness, shame, and humiliation. Self-compassion teaches you to acknowledge this pain without judging yourself for having it. Self-compassion also teaches you to show yourself the same mercy and kindness you would show someone else in the same situation. In the Introduction (p. xx), we talked about cultural norms in the Black community that tell us we have to always be strong no matter what. Unfortunately, this can cause us to suppress our feelings and prolong our suffering. Self-compassion can help to free you from this idea, allowing you to better honor and care for yourself.

In the Black community, there has been some stigma associated with mindfulness and meditation practices. Some people believe meditation involves subscribing to certain religious philosophies or communicating with spirits. Similarly, other people believe meditation is incompatible with prayer or reliance on God. While it is true that some types of meditation do have their origins in Eastern religious philosophies, meditation is a broad term that simply refers to non-judgmental attention to your thoughts, emotions, and physiological sensations. Thinking of meditation as awareness or even relaxation may help to ease some of these concerns if they apply to you. You can also look to your own religious texts to learn what they say about meditation and incorporate these ideas into your meditation practice (Watson-Singleton et al., 2019).

To use the self-compassion meditation script in the next section, you'll need some sort of audio recording device. Most smartphones come with a voice recording app that you can use. Use this meditation by first reading the meditation script that follows and then recording it on your device. Once you are ready to start the meditation, begin by first doing some diaphragmatic breathing, which is discussed in Activity 5, p. xx. Place one hand on your chest and one hand on your stomach, breathing in air through your nose and lungs so that your stomach pushes out, and breathing out through your mouth causing your stomach to suck in. Make sure you're sitting in a comfortable place and that your body is in a comfortable position. As you listen to your recording, you may want to have some soothing wordless music playing in the background to accompany this exercise. During the meditation, you may notice your thoughts drifting—that's ok. When this happens, simply bring your attention back to your breath and the words you are listening to. It may be helpful to also spend some time initially just observing your thoughts, watching them float by as if down a stream or on a cloud.

Self-Compassion Meditation Script

Close your eyes if this feels comfortable. Take a moment to notice your body. Then, notice your breathing.

(Pause)

Now, imagine yourself in a peaceful place. You can go to the beach, take a walk in a forest, or sit in a peaceful place in your home. Envision yourself in that place now.

Next, take a deep breath, breathing the air in through your nose and out through your mouth. Breathe in and out, nice and slow. Feel your chest slowly rise and fall. Each breath that you take is a healing and calming breath.

(Pause)

Scan your body for any tension. Notice any tension that might be in your body and gradually release that tension, relaxing your muscles.

(Pause)

Continue to take in nice healing breaths.

(Pause)

I want you now to bring your awareness to the place you have selected to go. Maybe you're at the beach or in the forest. Wherever you are, I want you to embrace the beauty and peacefulness of that place.

(Pause)

Use your senses and embrace everything you can hear, see, and perhaps even touch in this place.

(Pause)

As you are in this space, begin to send yourself these messages of compassion. Say silently to yourself:

"My experience with race hurts, but I am not alone."

(Pause)

"I am a survivor. I come from survivors."

(Pause)

"I am strong. My ancestors were strong. I am strong."

(Pause)

"I will love myself unconditionally."

(Pause)

Now, just listen.

Right now, in this moment, know that you matter.

Right now, in this moment, know that your presence is justified, and you do not need anyone to justify you.

Right now, in this moment, know that your presence is valued.

Right now, in this moment, know that you can be yourself.

In this moment there is safety.

You have value and worth.

(Pause)

As you move forward in your day, think of a person that represents strength for you. Embrace their strength and presence and move forward in the peace of this moment. You are deserving of this peace. You are not alone. Take a few more deep breaths and when you feel comfortable, open your eyes.

Additional Resources

If you'd like to try other meditations designed specifically for people of color, try:

- ❏ Black Girl in Om
- ❏ Black Zen
- ❏ Liberate Meditation
- ❏ The Black Lives Matter Meditation for Healing Racial Trauma

Reflection Questions

1. What was your experience with this meditation in general?

   _____

   _____

   _____

2. What sensations did you notice in your body during this meditation? How did these sensations change from the beginning to the end of the meditation?

   _____

   _____

   _____

3. What does self-compassion feel like in your body?

   _____

   _____

   _____

4. What else do you need to say to express compassion toward yourself?

   _____

   _____

   _____

5. How can self-compassion help you deal with your racialized trauma?

   _____

   _____

   _____

6. How will you know when you have developed self-compassion?

   _____

   _____

   _____

My Racial Healing Toolbox

In this part of the workbook, you learned several tools for healing from the wounds of racial trauma. Because racism is an ongoing issue in our society, it is likely that you will continue to be negatively affected by direct or indirect exposure to race-based incidents throughout your life. Therefore, being proactive and having a plan for self-care when confronted with these incidents is essential to the protection of your emotional and psychological wellbeing.

In Table 7.1 you will find a chart with two categories to describe the interventions discussed in the activities in this part. Under each category, identify your favorite tools from these activities and the situations in which it will be helpful to use them. Examples are provided for each category to help you get started. Be sure to refer back to your list as necessary.

TABLE 7.1

My Toolbox

Tool	Use
Cognitive Strategies **Example:** Positive self-talk	**Useful when...** Experiencing doubts or negative thoughts about myself
Mindfulness Strategies **Example:** Diaphragmatic breathing	**Useful when...** Experiencing anxiety or panic

PART 2

Tools to Promote Self-Esteem

DOI: 10.4324/9781003221357-10

When was the first time you really loved your Blackness? For Char, this did not happen until she was in her mid-20s and in grad school. Her love of herself and her Blackness came at this time because she was surrounded by Black professors who inspired her through their mentorship. Yet, as she reflects on this time in her life today, the fact that she did not develop this love for her Blackness until she was in her mid-20s is something that causes great sadness because of the time she lost not loving this part of herself. Similarly, Janeé also experiences a sense of sadness when she remembers the painful emotions she had concerning her Black identity as a small child; however, Janeé also experiences a great deal of pride and joy as she recalls the things that helped transform her negative view of herself as a Black person—things like participating in Black cultural events and being affirmed by others for her Black skin and hair. When thinking about your own journey with Black racial identity, it's likely that you too will experience a range of emotions. We asked a few of our friends and family about their memories of the first time they loved their Blackness. Here's what they had to say:

> When I was in elementary school, I was often made fun of because of my hair and I would be mixed up with other girls because we were all Black and all tall. I always wanted to be my own person and it was upsetting that people thought we all looked the same. I started to struggle with self-love and started comparing myself to others because I believed that if people didn't see the true me then why should I. It wasn't until the 10th grade that I really started to love myself for who I am as a Black girl, and this happened because of the people I met in my community, especially those who understood my struggle. Now I feel confident to express my true self and my passions.
>
> —Kamryn, age 16

> Seeing the movie *Malcolm X* and witnessing how Black celebrities came together with Spike Lee to fund the movie when White studios would not initially support the completion of the film made me feel proud as a Black man. Through Malcolm X's teachings about the strength of Black people and our history, I was able to believe that I could be greater than the little box they want us to live in. Because of that movie I understood that I came from more, so I could be more.
>
> —Van, age 45

> I never concentrated on my color. I have always felt like whatever I wanted to do I could do it. I grew up with every color, from Kindergarten to high school. We were all friends. I had White and Korean children that came to my house and I went to theirs. I feel like by being Black, I have a beautiful

color. I embrace what I have and have never felt like it was a hinderance to me. I embrace my color because I believe God gave it to me, so I've never been embarrassed about my color.

—Shirley, age 81

As illustrated in these stories, there are indeed a variety of feelings that occur in the process of developing a positive racial identity; however, with the right experiences and support, we are typically able to develop a positive view of ourselves as racial beings, which research shows is strongly connected to our self-esteem (Pieterse et al., 2012). A healthy sense of self-esteem is something everyone needs to feel secure and have positive relationships with others. It also influences our choices and motivates us to do well in life. Because of this, it is important that we learn how to nurture and protect our self-esteem.

In this part of the workbook, we define healthy self-esteem, describe its benefits, and discuss the impact of racism and negative societal messages on self-esteem within the Black community. The activities in this part are designed to help you assess your self-esteem, affirm your personal strengths, increase positive self-talk, and encourage racial and ethnic pride. We also focus on helping you to identify, challenge, and replace negative beliefs and stereotypes about Black people, with the goal of developing counternarratives to protect against internalized racism and other challenges to healthy self-esteem.

What is Self-Esteem?

So, what exactly is self-esteem? *Self-esteem* is defined as an individual's view of their self-worth (Rosenberg, 1979). Individuals with healthy self-esteem have greater confidence, perseverance, problem-solving ability, and body positivity. They also experience more positive life outcomes including greater educational attainment, professional success, and overall psychological well-being. For African Americans, healthy self-esteem additionally serves as a protective factor when coping with racism and shame resulting from racist events (Johnson, 2020). Beyond this, high self-esteem can help buffer against internalized racism, which refers to belief in negative stereotypes about one's racial group that turn into negative thoughts about oneself, like not being good enough.

Interestingly, research suggests that African Americans generally have good self-esteem. In fact, decades of studies have even found that African Americans generally have higher self-esteem than their White peers (Patterson, 2004). We know that this may seem confusing given what you learned earlier in this workbook about internalized racism and anti-Black attitudes, but there is a logical explanation. While Black people who are dealing with internalized racism do feel inferior when compared to White people, self-esteem is generally developed as we compare ourselves to people in our immediate environments (Hughes & Demo, 1989). This means that we develop our self-esteem as a result of how we relate to our family, friends, church, and community members, people who tend to look like us, not in comparison to White people. Moreover, research additionally shows that this is especially true for Black women who tend to support each other by validating each other's experiences, thoughts, and feelings (Eugene, 1995). Essentially, Black women are good at hyping each other up and this type of social support helps to protect against the negative effects of racism that might otherwise result in low self-esteem (Patterson, 2004).

Beyond social support, many researchers have found that racial socialization is another positive factor in the development of healthy self-esteem, especially as it relates to protection against racism. *Racial socialization* can be defined as "behaviors, communications, and interactions that address how African Americans ought to feel about their cultural heritage and how they should respond to the racial hostility or confusion in American society" (Brown, 2008, p. 33). We'll talk about racial socialization in more depth in Part 3: Tools to Promote Resilience; however, we thought it was important to bring it up now, given its connection to self-esteem. According to Okeke-Adeyanju et al. (2014), the primary themes of racial socialization include cultural pride, preparation for bias, egalitarianism, self-worth, and responding appropriately to negative messages. Racial socialization through *cultural pride* involves communicating messages that highlight the history, strengths, and accomplishments of African Americans. *Preparation for bias* involves gaining the skills necessary to handle and cope

Don't Forget Your Crown

Famous poet Maya Angelou once said, "Your crown has been bought and paid for. Put it on your head and wear it." Depending on your perspective, this quote may have different meanings. When some people hear this quote, they think of the ancestors who died during slavery and the Civil Rights Era so that we could have a better life. Other people are reminded of Africa's history of great civilizations and that as a people, we are descendants of kings and queens. Still others with Christian beliefs are reminded that because of Jesus's sacrifice on the cross, we are now joint heirs with Christ, children of the King of all kings.

What comes to mind for you when you hear this quote? Our hope is that you see yourself as royalty, someone who should be loved, honored, and cherished. Yet, we know sometimes life can get overwhelming and it can be hard to see yourself that way. If you've "forgotten your crown," here are a few things you can do to remember it:

❏ Focus on what makes you special
❏ Spend time taking care of yourself
❏ Help others

with negative race-based encounters. *Egalitarianism* involves working toward racial equality, while *self-worth* focuses on one's view of self. Lastly, *responding appropriately to negative messages* refers to the development of strategies to challenge and eliminate stereotyped views of African Americans in one's thinking (Okeke-Adeyanju et al., 2014). The more we integrate these themes into our lives, the stronger our racial identity becomes, which in turn leads to healthier self-esteem.

We Know It's Called Self-Esteem, But...

As we've discussed, self-esteem is generally defined as an individual's view of their self-worth; however, something called collective self-esteem is also important to the development of a positive racial identity and a healthy sense of individual self-esteem. *Collective self-esteem* can be defined as an aspect of self-esteem that comes from a person's connection to their social group (Barrie et al., 2016). As it relates to racial identity, this includes valuing your place in the Black community and feeling emotionally connected to other members of this group.

Like individual self-esteem, research shows that collective self-esteem protects against depression, anxiety, and physical distress when confronted with racial discrimination (Fischer & Holz, 2007). Moreover, research conducted by Barrie et al. (2016) has also found that moderate to high levels of collective self-esteem can decrease the internalization of negative racial stereotypes. This means that collective self-esteem not only minimizes the harmful psychological effects of racial discrimination, but it also minimizes the extent to which we apply anti-Black messages to ourselves.

One of our favorite fictional examples of how collective self-esteem works is the movie *Waiting to Exhale.* Featuring an all-Black cast, this movie was a cultural phenomenon at the time of its release, opening at number one in the North American box office and grossing $14.1 million over its first weekend ("Waiting to Exhale," 2022). Part of what made this movie such as success, especially in the African American community, was that it featured many of the best parts of Black culture. It was funny and irreverent, the characters were complex, intelligent, successful, and beautiful, and the soundtrack was hot! And yet above all this, the main thing that made this movie so valuable is that at its core, *Waiting to Exhale* highlighted the love and support African Americans show each other as they navigate difficulties in romance, work, and family relationships. It reminded us of the strength and healing we can find when we care for one another.

Okay. So, we know *Waiting to Exhale* was a long time ago, and maybe you never saw that movie. Another more recent movie highlighting collective self-esteem is the film *Black Panther*. In *Black Panther*, King T'Challa is ruler over a fictional African kingdom known as Wakanda. Wakanda is a technologically advanced nation replete with natural resources the people use to serve and protect their physical environment and each other. Like *Waiting to Exhale*, the characters in *Black Panther* were funny, powerful, and intelligent, and the movie was another cultural phenomenon because it reminded us of the strength, beauty, and swag we have as a people. As you think about *Waiting to Exhale*, *Black Panther*, or one of your own favorite movies, what comes to your mind in terms of the role of collective self-esteem in your own life? Perhaps there are small ways you demonstrate collective self-esteem in your everyday life that you may be overlooking. For example, if you've ever used sayings like, "I'm Black and I'm proud," "Black power," "Black excellence," "Black girl magic," "Black boy joy," "Love a Black woman from infinity to infinity," or even "Wakanda forever," you've demonstrated collective self-esteem. While these small affirmations may seem insignificant, they offer a powerful psychological boost, especially when it comes to challenging negative stereotypes and discrimination.

One Last Thing

While research shows that self-esteem is connected to various life outcomes and protects against racism, research also suggests that even when some Black people have high self-esteem, they may nevertheless have low self-efficacy. *Self-efficacy* refers to one's belief in their ability to perform certain tasks or reach certain goals (American Psychological Association, n.d. c). Self-efficacy is important because people with low self-efficacy are less likely to set goals for themselves or to persist when faced with obstacles to their goals. One of the most compelling studies of self-esteem and self-efficacy among Black people found that while these two constructs are related, self-efficacy is unique in that it is strongly influenced by social class and opportunities to experience oneself as powerful and autonomous

Representation Matters

In this section, we discussed the importance of self-efficacy beliefs and the fact that self-efficacy can be lowered when people have few opportunities to experience themselves as powerful and autonomous (Hughes & Demo, 1989). Research also shows, however, that self-efficacy is additionally impacted by the absence of people who look like us in positions of power (Hackett & Byars, 1996). Therefore, being intentional in exposing ourselves to examples of Black people who are successful in all fields and spheres of life can be a powerful way to positive influence our own sense of self-efficacy. Try it yourself! Start by writing down two careers or spheres of life in which, according to stereotypes, Black people do not do well. Then, use Google or your favorite research tool to find at least two people who counter this stereotype. Journal about your findings and how they make you feel about yourself.

(Hughes & Demo, 1989). In other words, to some extent, people develop self-efficacy as they experience success in the areas of life that grant status, for example, in their careers, the neighborhoods they live in, etc. For Black people, the ability to achieve higher levels of social status is often hindered by discrimination, as discrimination limits access to power and resources that afford individuals the best opportunities to experience themselves as powerful and autonomous (Hughes & Demo, 1989). Therefore, as we think about racial influences on how we see ourselves and our futures, we don't want to overlook the importance of discrimination and self-efficacy in our overall self-concept. Accordingly, activities in this part focus on our ability to set and achieve goals in addition to ways we can develop and enhance our self-esteem.

Self-Esteem Questionnaire

Previously, we defined *self-esteem* as an individual's view of their self-worth (Rosenberg, 1979). Based on this definition, another way to think of self-esteem is how much we like ourselves regardless of what's going on in our lives (Cherry, 2021). For example, people with a healthy sense of self-esteem are generally able to bounce back from mistakes or hardships without being overly critical or down on themselves. People with poor self-esteem, on the other hand, tend to use mistakes and difficulties as evidence to support pre-existing negative beliefs about themselves. Even when they haven't experienced any difficulties, people with poor self-esteem generally tend to live in ways that reinforce their negative self-perceptions by doing things like being self-critical, discounting the positives, and engaging in behaviors that may be harmful or against their values in order to receive love or approval from others. Understanding the difference between healthy and poor self-esteem can help you to ensure that you are taking the steps necessary to maintain a positive view of yourself. It can also help to protect your mental health and your view of yourself when you are confronted by racial discrimination or harassment.

According to psychologist Kendra Cherry (2021), self-esteem consists of many factors, some of which include self-confidence, a feeling of security, a clearly defined identity, a sense of belonging, and a feeling of competence. The American Psychological Association has a really useful dictionary that helps us to understand the meaning of these terms. *Self-confidence* is defined as having trust and a positive attitude about your abilities, capabilities, and judgment. *Security* refers to a sense of safety and freedom. One of the most important ways we gain security is by having accepting friends and family. Your *identity* refers to how you see yourself as a person. It is mostly defined by a combination of two things—the characteristics that make you unique (for example, your personality, physical appearance, and interests) and your group affiliations and social roles (for example, your race, gender, gender expression, what you do for a career, being a parent, being a religious leader, etc.). *Belonging* refers to how much you feel personally accepted, respected, included, and supported by others in your environment (Goodenow & Grady, 1993). Finally, *competence* refers to the ability to do something successfully or efficiently. From a psychological perspective, this includes the ability to exert control over your life, to cope with problems effectively, and to make changes in your behavior or environment when needed. If you are interested in reading more about these terms or other psychological concepts, you can visit the APA dictionary by going to: https://dictionary.apa.org/

This activity is designed to help you reflect on your self-esteem and identify specific areas for growth. Begin by completing the following questionnaire. Read the statements and rate yourself on a scale that ranges from 1 = *strongly disagree* to 5 = *strongly agree*, as each statement applies to you. Next, use the reflection questions to help you explore the meaning of your responses to the statements on the questionnaire. Based on your reflections, complete this activity by identifying specific habits you can begin to either develop or enhance in each of the areas of self-esteem we've discussed.

Self-Esteem Questionnaire

1 = Strongly Disagree; 2 = Disagree; 3 = Neutral; 4 = Agree; 5 = Strongly Agree

1. I can accomplish my goals and make good decisions for myself.   1   2   3   4   5

2. I have worth regardless of my beliefs or the choices I make.   1   2   3   4   5

3. I like my personality, the way I look, and the groups I belong to.   1   2   3   4   5

4. I believe I'm important to my friends and family.   1   2   3   4   5

5. I have the ability to do things well and accomplish my goals.   1   2   3   4   5

Reflection Questions

We hope that you were able to answer 5 to all of the questions in the questionnaire; however, it's more likely that some aspects of your self-esteem are strong, while other aspects of your self-esteem may be areas for continued growth. In the short questionnaire, items 1, 2, 3, 4, and 5 correspond to self-confidence, security, identity, belonging, and competence, respectively. Think about your responses to each item as you respond to the reflection questions that follow.

1. What are your strongest areas of self-esteem? Which areas of your self-esteem need further growth?

_____

_____

_____

2. When is your self-esteem highest?

_____

_____

_____

3. When do you struggle with your self-esteem?

_____

_____

_____

4. What positive things can you say to yourself when you are struggling with your self-esteem?

_____

_____

_____

Develop a Plan

Finally, as suggested by the last reflection question, positive self-talk can have a big impact on your self-esteem over time. However, there are other things you can do to support the development of a healthy self-esteem as well. For example, practicing self-compassion, spending time with people who make you happy, and eating right and exercising are all effective strategies for boosting your self-esteem. Having a plan and being intentional about including these types of activities in your life is a great first step when it comes to nurturing and enhancing your view of yourself. In what follows, we've listed these and a few other strategies you can use to feel better about yourself. Try them out for a week. Circle the activities that seem interesting to you, and then commit to practicing at least one of these activities every day. Write the activities you selected and journal about your thoughts and feelings in the space provided.

My Self-Esteem Strategies

- ❏ Say no to negative self-talk
- ❏ Exercise
- ❏ Eat more fruits and vegetables
- ❏ Go for a walk in nature
- ❏ Use positive self-affirmations
- ❏ Help someone else
- ❏ Read something inspirational
- ❏ Try a new skincare, makeup, or haircare routine
- ❏ Surround yourself with positive people
- ❏ Try a loving-kindness meditation
- ❏ Focus on your skills and abilities
- ❏ Learn a new skill
- ❏ List your accomplishments
- ❏ Develop your own view of success
- ❏ Others: _____

My Self-Esteem Plan

Monday

Activity: _____

My thoughts and feelings: _____

_____

_____

_____

Tuesday

Activity: _____

My thoughts and feelings: _____

_____

_____

_____

Wednesday

Activity: _____

My thoughts and feelings: _____

_____

_____

_____

Thursday

Activity: _____

My thoughts and feelings: _____

_____

_____

_____

Friday

Activity: _____

My thoughts and feelings: _____

_____

_____

_____

Saturday

Activity: _____

My thoughts and feelings: _____

_____

_____

_____

Sunday

Activity: _____

My thoughts and feelings: _____

_____

_____

_____

Black Racial Identity Quiz

In the Introduction to this workbook, we discussed the nigrescence model, a theory of Black racial identity development originated by leading researcher and psychologist, Dr. William Cross Jr. (1991, 1995). Recall that the model consists of four stages: pre-encounter, encounter, immersion/emersion, and internalization. Through taking the quiz in Table 9.1 you can get an idea where you are at in regard to these stages. If a statement is True, place a checkmark under the column labeled "T." If a statement is False, place a checkmark in the column labeled "F."

TABLE 9.1
Black Racial Identity Quiz

Questions	T	F
1. To be "White is right" and "Black is wrong."		
2. I often seek acceptance from White people.		
3. I believe White culture is more beautiful than Black culture.		
4. I have few Black friends.		
5. I see my racial group membership as one that is targeted by racism.		
6. I feel forced to acknowledge racism because of events that have occurred in society.		
7. I desire to surround myself with visible symbols of my Black racial identity.*		
8. I actively avoid symbols of Whiteness.		
9. I actively seek out opportunities to explore aspects of my own history and culture with the support of members from my own racial background.*		
10. I seek to establish meaningful relationships with Whites who acknowledge and are respectful of my racial identity.*		
11. I feel I have a positive sense of self as it relates to my Black identity.*		
12. I have a plan of action or a general sense of commitment to address concerns of Black people.*		

Reflection Questions

Now, we'd like you to take a moment to reflect on the questions to which you answered "True" by responding to the following questions.

1. What do you notice about your answers? Do they reflect a sense of Black pride?

_____

_____

_____

_____

_____

_____

_____

_____

_____

2. What experiences may have impacted your answers?

_____

_____

_____

_____

_____

_____

_____

_____

_____

_____

Finally, take a moment and look at the statements that have an asterisk (*) next to them and see if you marked them as true. These statements are more in line with positive Black identity. If you notice you did not endorse a lot of the statements that are connected with a high sense of confidence and a positive sense of Black racial identity, it might be good to go back and revisit the section of this workbook that looks at racial healing (see pp. 21–68). The activities within the Racial Healing section may help you develop a plan for moving forward with a more positive sense of self.

Bonus: Researcher Blakesley (2016) proposed several strategies that Black people can use to unlearn and resist anti-Black attitudes and internalized racism on the way to developing a more positive racial identity. The following list gives some ideas from her research. Take a moment and place a check in the boxes for the items you could do to enhance your own racial identity.

- ❑ Work on projects in your personal life that provide you with meaning and purpose
- ❑ Challenge internalized racism in self and others by affirming your Black identities through positive self-talk
- ❑ Find Black role models
- ❑ Seek Black mentors
- ❑ Challenge beauty standards by just being you instead of conforming
- ❑ Participate in a course that is geared toward raising racial consciousness and pride
- ❑ Seek out images that validate your experiences as a Black person (e.g., Black magazines and/or books)

Your Melanin is Poppin'

Appreciation of our Black bodies is crucial to building self-esteem. The media will have us believe that Black bodies are not beautiful, but this is not the truth. Everything about you is beautiful, starting with your skin. As they say, "Your melanin is poppin'!"

The phrase, "Your melanin is poppin'" is another one of those sayings that is meant to build us up, and with good reason. Melanin is the substance in your body that produces your hair, eye, and skin color (Cleveland Clinic, n.d.). Its primary function is to protect your cells from sun damage. People from sunnier regions tend to have more melanin, which is the reason why people with African ancestry usually have darker skin. Yet, in spite of this simple scientific explanation for dark skin, darker skin has been equated to less physical attractiveness and desirability. Telling yourself or someone else that your melanin is poppin' is a way to challenge negative societal attitudes toward Black skin and to affirm its beauty.

Negative views toward Black skin are a remnant of slavery and the White supremacy that was developed during this time. Unfortunately, these views to some extent have become internalized within the Black community, especially as it relates to colorism and skin dissatisfaction. *Colorism* is the unequal treatment of individuals based on the lightness or darkness of their skin tone (Landor & Smith, 2019). This treatment can be between individuals or within systems. Actor Charlie Murphy's story of singer Rick James calling Charlie and his brother Eddie Murphy "twin darknesses" is a humorous but nonetheless sad and common example of how ridicule based on skin color can occur between individuals. It's likely that you are able to recall examples of this from your own childhood. Perhaps some of your friends with dark skin were called ugly, or maybe you saw friends with light skin being accused of thinking they were better than others or bullied for not being Black enough. These experiences can be emotionally and psychologically distressing and may even lead to what Landor and Smith (2019) call skin-tone trauma.

Healing from skin-tone trauma or just appreciating your skin complexion if skin-tone trauma has not been a factor in your life can boost your self-esteem and increase your confidence in yourself. In this activity, we focus on learning to appreciate our skin and parts of our bodies.

Reflection Questions

We come from a long line of beautiful people. Take a moment and reflect on some of your beautiful ancestors—these can be people you know or people you do not know. In the following space provided, write about what makes them beautiful to you. Maybe it's the glow of their skin or their flawless complexion. Jot down whatever you think makes them pop.

_____

_____

_____

_____

Now, take a moment and reflect on what about you makes your own melanin pop. In essence, what do you think makes your skin and complexion beautiful?

_____

_____

_____

_____

Women and Men Are Both Affected

Beyond our skin complexion, it is also important that we learn how to love the other aspects of our physical bodies. This is especially important now, as newer research indicates that Black people are beginning to experience body dissatisfaction at rates similar to their White counterparts (Dunn et al., 2019). Whereas Black women were previously found to generally have positive body images, newer data suggests that not only are Black women experiencing an uptick in body dissatisfaction, but they are also beginning to experience more shame in connection with their bodies (Talleyrand et al., 2017). Likewise, while the research on Black men and body image is more limited, data suggests that this group of individuals also struggles with how they view and appreciate their bodies, particularly as it relates to physical strength and masculinity (Osa & Kelly, 2021).

Body appreciation can be defined as an individual's acceptance of and respect for their body regardless of how their body fits societal body standards (Dunn et al., 2019, p. 121). Many factors influence body appreciation. Among Black women, preferences for body ideals with proximity to Whiteness such as light skin, "good" hair, and a curvy yet slender body shape, all influence the extent to which Black women feel good about their bodies (Stephens & Few, 2007). Gendered stereotypes and standards that sexually objectify Black women also have an impact on how Black women value their bodies. For example, within the Black community, women are expected to be "thick," which depending on the context may simply be a description of a woman's body type, but it is often a connotation of their sexual desirability. According to researcher Kamille Gentles-Peart (2018), thickness can be defined as "a voluptuous [B]lack female body with ample derriere, hips, and thighs" (p. 200). While a preference for thickness in some ways protects against a poor body image based on Eurocentric preferences for thinner body types, it also leads to body dissatisfaction for Black women who do not have a thick body type (Hughes, 2021) and may even lead to a desire among women with thick body types to become thicker and curvier, causing both groups of women to take unhealthy and sometimes drastic measures like opting for a Brazilian butt lift (BBL), which has the highest death rate of all cosmetic surgeries (Ellin, 2021), to achieve this ideal.

Gendered stereotypes and standards may also influence Black men's perceptions of their body image, as these men are impacted by traditional gender norms which suggest that increased muscularity equates to greater masculinity and power as a man. Interestingly, Black men's desire for muscularity, while part of traditional gender norms, may also be influenced by discrimination. According to research conducted by Osa and Kelly (2021), African

American men who reported more experiences with discrimination were also found to have a greater drive for muscularity. Building on previous studies, the researchers explained their findings by noting that discrimination is at its core disempowering and can lead to feelings of helplessness. Masculinity as achieved through muscularity may be a coping strategy Black men use to protect themselves from these emasculating effects of racial discrimination. Moreover, Osa and Kelly (2021) also note that ethnic identity did not lessen the relationship between discrimination and drive for muscularity. This is significant as ethnic identity is typically found to protect against body image issues among African American women. Osa and Kelly's (2021) research shows that this may be the case for African American men.

So, what does this all mean for you as the average person? Well, the research concerning factors influencing body appreciation have several implications for both men and women. First, it is important that both men and women realize that some of their ideas concerning body image come from unfair societal expectations. Instead of striving to meet these expectations, which are not only unfair but in some cases are impossible, it is important that we develop self-defined standards of beauty focused on health and wellness. Second, because body appreciation can be impacted by our relationships with others, it is also important that we resist putting unfair expectations and judgments onto our friends and family. Rather than critique others for being "bony," "skinny," "big-boned," or any of the other terms we may use, it would be more helpful for us to keep our opinions to ourselves. Generally, labeling or criticizing others doesn't help. It usually just makes them feel anxious or bad about themselves. Finally, no matter how we feel at a certain point in time, we're all human and we're all vulnerable to the things we hear and see. Therefore, try to be careful about what you view and listen to. Work to fill yourself with messages that are positive and build you up rather than tear you down.

Show Yourself Some Love

Earlier we mentioned that perceptions of body image are changing in the Black community. Prior to the 2000s, body images based on thin Eurocentric ideals were widely recognized as racist and based in White supremacy. In fact, larger heavier body types were often praised for their strength and presence, and celebration of larger body sizes could even be viewed as a sign of resistance to racial and gender oppression (Allan et al., 1993; Cameron et al., 2018). An unfortunate side effect of these attitudes, however, is that they may have contributed to the epidemics of high blood pressure, diabetes, and obesity in the Black community. Today, members of the Black community are becoming increasingly conscious of the connection between body size and health, which is a good thing; however, this increased consciousness may also include an increased sense of inner conflict, self-criticism, and shame associated with weight (Talleyrand et al., 2017; Watson et al., 2013).

We want to encourage you to be balanced in how you view your body. Health is important but everyone is beautiful regardless of their size or the extent to which they meet society's standards of the perfect body. The following list gives some specific steps that can foster body appreciation. Read the steps and circle the ones you would benefit from doing more of in your daily life.

❏ **Extend grace to your body.** Our bodies go through a lot of stress due to racism and other stressors in everyday life. We need to learn to appreciate and extend compassion ourselves. Extending grace may look like accepting flaws or imperfections in your body. Extending grace also entails being kind to your body by eating healthier foods, drinking a healthy amount of water, and exercising.

❏ **Don't compare yourself to White images.** It's easy to compare ourselves to images of the dominant culture, but this can cause us to miss our own value. Don't let your measurement of yourself be based on how you compare yourself to others because you will miss out on what makes you shine.

❏ **Ground your body.** Allow for moments in your day where you can just appreciate yourself, perhaps by sitting in silence and just feeling your feet on the floor. Allow yourself to connect with your body by just being present in the moment.

❏ **Appreciate your Blackness.** Think of things that allow you to show confidence in your Black identity. The latter may look like wearing a sweatshirt with a phrase that celebrates your Black identity or perhaps one from a historically Black college. Appreciating your Blackness may even be deciding to rock your own natural hair...think of what works for you!

Beyond Skin Deep

Finally, as we conclude this exploration of body appreciation, we want to remind you that while appreciation of your physical attractiveness can help your self-esteem, ultimately, physical beauty is only skin deep. Some of the things that make us beautiful are not our physical appearance but our internal characteristics. Therefore, as you complete this activity, we invite you to engage in one final activity that invites you to reflect on your whole person, both inside and out. Complete the following sentences, and as you do, feel free to respond however you'd like, whether it's based on how you look or some aspect of your personality. The only requirement is that you honor and value who you are as a person.

1. Something that makes me unique is

   _____

   _____

   _____

   _____

   _____

2. My strengths are

   _____

   _____

   _____

   _____

3. Something I love about myself is

   _____

   _____

   _____

   _____

   _____

4. One of the things I love most about being Black is

_____

_____

_____

_____

_____

5. I shine because I

_____

_____

_____

_____

_____

6. I show respect for myself by

_____

_____

_____

_____

_____

7. Positive adjectives that best describe who I am and what I am about are

_____

_____

_____

_____

_____

Let Your Social Media Reflect Your Confidence

Social media is one of those things in life that's like a double-edged sword. On the one hand, social media allows us to showcase our talents and accomplishments, stay close to family, and reconnect with long lost friends. These qualities of social media can enhance our lives, and even our pockets for those of us who are able to build businesses, advertise, obtain endorsements, or become influencers through social media.

On the other hand, social media can also cause us to feel bad about ourselves. For example, we may see people on social media who appear to be doing better in life than we are and feel inferior in comparison. Moreover, social media can also be a source of psychological distress when we are exposed to images of violence or racism against Black people. For example, individuals who see police killings online often experience vicarious trauma severe enough to meet criteria for an anxiety disorder or PTSD (Ramsden, 2017), and racial minorities who are exposed to racism online may engage in risky behaviors like alcohol use to cope with stress (Keum & Cano, 2021).

Social Media Tips

Because social media is somewhat new, the depth of its effects on the Black community are not known. Yet, from the research that does exist, as well as stories from our own clinical experiences, it's clear that social media is something we should all think about when it comes to protecting our self-esteem. The following list gives some tips to protect and build your self-esteem by controlling your use of social media. Take a moment to read through the list and circle the things you can do to further help your self-esteem development.

- ❑ **Don't filter.** There are a lot of apps and software that allow for people to filter their image. Start posting pictures of yourself without filters so you get more comfortable with your natural beauty and who you are authentically.
- ❑ **Block negativity.** Take a moment and go through your social media to block people or groups that do not enrich you or your mindset. Negativity can pull down how we see ourselves and make us feel inadequate, anxious, or depressed. It can also cause isolation, loss of sleep, and fear of missing out. Keep yourself safe from images that will lower your self-esteem.
- ❑ **Pay someone a compliment.** Sometimes going outside of ourselves and speaking kindness into another person's life can help us feel good. The compliment may even be reciprocated, which is an added bonus!
- ❑ **Celebrate you.** Don't be afraid to post your accomplishments no matter how big or small. You've worked hard, so it's ok to give yourself a shout out every now and then.
- ❑ **Log off.** Set a limit for the amount of time you spend on social media. Too much time can take you away from nurturing other parts of yourself.
- ❑ **Find social media groups that support your racial identity or heritage.** As we mentioned, social media can be positive when used appropriately. There are many social media groups you can join in order to be part of a community that will affirm your identity or help you accomplish your goals. These groups may be entirely social in nature, or they may consist of professionals of your same race. Whatever type of group you join, make sure the group is a space where you can get validation, resources, and support.

Check Yourself

Finally, as you read through the list and identify ways to protect your self-esteem while using social media, be sure to also be mindful of social media's effect on your attitude toward others. Certain social media platforms can be full of toxic content. Over time, exposure to this content can cause us to be angry, critical, sarcastic, or antagonistic in our own views toward others. Researchers call this type of behavior *emotional contagion* and find that while most social media posts are positive in nature, individuals tend to be more affected by posts that arouse highly negative emotions such as anger, hate, or outrage (Hsu et al., 2021). These emotions in turn lead to "anger bandwagons," "viral online shaming," and polarization or divisions among groups of people (Hsu et al., 2021, p. 970). You can avoid engaging in these behaviors by conducting regular checks of your emotional space as you use social media by asking yourself the following questions. You'll feel better if you do!

- ❏ **How do I feel after using social media?** If you tend to feel anger or some other distressing emotion after using social media, it may be time to make some changes to either the amount of time you spend on social media or the type of content you are viewing.
- ❏ **What kinds of posts tend to come across my newsfeed or For You page?** If you are seeing negative posts online, it's likely that they are being directed toward you because you spend more time engaged with those types of posts. Interrupt the cycle by intentionally seeking out content that is positive and uplifting in nature.
- ❏ **Are my comments something I would say to someone in a face-to-face conversation?** The anonymity of social media can give people permission to say things they would not normally say to someone in person. Remember to govern yourself according to your values while in online spaces. Being a person of integrity always has a positive effect on your self-esteem.

Take a Selfie

We hope you haven't forgotten our suggestion for you to stop and take a break every once in a while as you move through this workbook. In case you have, here's a reminder and a fun way to do so. In this activity, we want to encourage you to have some fun practicing self-love by taking a selfie. Self-love is crucial to wellness and living your best life. When we love ourselves, we are able to overcome negativity and be confident in who we are. Accordingly, this activity involves you connecting with and complimenting your natural self. We ask that you remove any make-up or anything you use to enhance your beauty. Once removed, your task is to take a picture of yourself and then take a moment to look at your picture. While looking at your picture, pay yourself five compliments about your natural beauty and write them in the following space. Ready? Say, cheese!

1. _____
2. _____
3. _____
4. _____
5. _____

As you look at your list, remember these are just some of the things that make you beautiful. You are beautiful inside and out!

Family Ties

One of the books that has had the greatest impact on our understanding of healing from racial trauma is called *My Grandmother's Hands: Racialized Trauma and the Pathway to Mending Our Hearts and Bodies* (Menakem, 2017). If you have not read it, we highly recommend it. In this book, noted trauma expert Resmaa Menakem discusses the racial crisis in the United States, how this crisis has resulted in trauma within the Black community, and ways Black people can heal from this trauma. Among some of his most profound ideas are his comments on how some of the ideas and behaviors we have as African Americans may actually be responses to trauma that we've forgotten to acknowledge over time and have instead blamed on our individual personalities, families, or culture. According to Menakem (2017), examples of these responses include self-hate, internalized racism, a bias for light skin over dark skin, a preference for shopping in White-owned businesses, and denigration of other African Americans who have achieved success (p. 167).

Another way of thinking about Menakem's (2017) work is in terms of transgenerational trauma. *Transgenerational trauma* is defined as the impact of traumatic experiences, not only on one generation but on subsequent generations (Bryant-Davis et al., 2017). It includes the by-product of traumatic events like racism that get passed down from one generation to the next. For example, racism allowed slavery to occur, which forced us to be separated from our homeland and our roots, which caused us to be stripped from parts of our identity, which ultimately resulted in the suppression of our culture. This type of trauma is significant not only because of the emotional and psychological pain it causes, but also because of the harm it can cause to our view of ourselves.

Some have argued that transgenerational trauma caused by colonialism, American slavery, segregation, and discrimination has impacted the self-worth and psychological wellbeing of Black people so much so that it has created a mentality that is rooted in inferiority (Barlow, 2018). While this idea is certainly debatable, it's clear that messages of inferiority that have been passed down through generations have some effect on our behavior and how we see ourselves. Next we discuss the case of Jeremy, a pseudonym for a volunteer who was willing to share his story using a transgenerational trauma family tree to illustrate what transgenerational trauma might look like in an individual's life. After you read Jeremy's story, we invite you to complete your own family tree to explore how transgenerational trauma has affected your own life.

The Case of Jeremy

Jeremy grew up in a family in which his great-grandparents, grandparents, and parents were raised in poverty. When his family did come into a little bit of money, the family would often spend the money instead of saving or investing it. The message that Jeremy learned from his family is that "Money is to be spent."

As an adult, Jeremy now has his own family, including two children. He finds himself repeating some of the same financial struggles of his family of origin. During tax season, Jeremy typically receives tax refunds equating to several thousand dollars. Instead of investing the money to help his family, he chooses to spend the money on designer clothes, eating out, and fancy rims for his car. He repeats the family message, "Money is to be spent," but ends up feeling depressed and worthless due to being financially broke yet again.

Johnson Side of the Family
Grandmother was a single mother who faced sexism and discrimination as a Black woman. When she would get extra money from cleaning homes, she spent it quickly and often on things she did not need. Grandfather was absent from the home, so Jeremy never saw the economic influence of having a two parent home.

Newberry Side of the Family
Grandmother and grandfather were rather cold and distant due to experiencing discrimination and racism in their blue collar jobs. They were born in the midst of Jim Crow era where opportunities were limited. They never talked about money or anything but expressed stress due to racism and living in poverty. Jeremy learned that children are "to be seen and not heard." Jeremy missed out on learning about how to manage money and avoid financial issues.

The figure here shows Jeremy's transgenerational trauma tree. Jeremy was only able to go back to his grandparents because he did not know his great-grandparents. As you can see, Jeremy traced his transgenerational trauma back to issues in his family that stemmed from Jim Crow, discrimination, and broken family relationships. While reading about Jeremy's family history of trauma, keep in mind that not only did this trauma reinforce a cycle of poverty in his life but it also lowered his self-esteem by eliciting feelings of helplessness and powerlessness, which as we discussed in Activity 10 can be particularly painful for Black men whose self-esteem is also connected to their masculinity and ability to provide for their families.

Your Story of Transgenerational Trauma

Now that you've read Jeremy's story of transgenerational trauma, take a moment to think of your own story. In what ways have negative family or cultural patterns impacted your sense of self-esteem or self-worth? In the blank family tree, list key family members and identify how transgenerational trauma may have been passed to you through these family members. Then, respond to the reflection questions to help you further process the impact of this trauma in your life.

Reflection Questions

1. What negative messages or limiting beliefs did you receive from your family as a result of transgenerational trauma?

_____

_____

_____

2. What impact has racism had on your family trauma?

_____

_____

_____

Breaking Transgenerational Trauma

For Jeremy, breaking his transgenerational trauma requires first recognizing his pattern of spending as being a trauma response. Once Jeremy has identified this pattern, he may then decide that the messages he has been given about money are problematic. He can then begin to think of ways to invest his money or save his money, which would result in him feeling empowered and have a positive effect on his self-esteem.

In the following space provided, look at your family tree and the unhealthy messages given to you across generations. Write about how you can change some of these unhealthy messages and behavioral patterns in order to create a healthier sense of self.

_____

_____

_____

_____

_____

_____

_____

_____

Proud Moments

Recently, Disney+ revived the animated television series, *The Proud Family*. The series originally aired between 2001 and 2005, so, depending on your age, the age of your children, or your interest in animated television, you may have seen this show either during its original run or in its current reboot. The show features Penny Proud, a 14-year-old African American girl, and her family members, depicting the love and support they have for each other as they experience funny, everyday life situations. Part of what makes this show such a success is that it illustrates just how powerful the Black family can be in developing the esteem and confidence of its members. The show's theme song even reinforces this idea with lyrics focused on the ability to be oneself around family members more than anyone else. In fact, according to the song, this is characteristic—that is, being held in high esteem just for being you—of what actually makes a family, a family.

In the prior activity, you explored how family, through transgenerational trauma, can be a source of attitudes and behaviors that ultimately lead to low self-esteem. While it is true that family can at times be a source of factors that diminish your self-esteem, it is also true that family can be a source of pride that contributes to healthy self-esteem. In fact, researchers find that families can be a primary source of self-esteem among African Americans, especially in the face of adversities like racism. This is because African American families are often intentional in teaching their children to love and believe in themselves by having racial and ethnic pride and by embracing their family heritage, which results in a greater sense of confidence and competence, some of the most significant factors in overall self-esteem (Littlejohn-Blake & Darling, 1993).

In this activity, we invite you to reflect on proud family moments in your own life. We begin by sharing some of our proud family moments and what these moments mean for us. We then ask you to write down your own proud family moments and what these moments mean for you. We hope that by doing so, you find another way to affirm how special and important you are.

Dr. Char's Proud Family Moments

One of my proud family moments was seeing pictures of my maternal grandparents as they marched with Dr. Martin Luther King. These pictures help me feel proud because they showed me that my grandparents were brave individuals who believed in fighting for what was right. Another proud family moment of mine was learning that my paternal grandfather was instrumental in helping to organize one of the prominent Black churches in Detroit, Michigan. As a teenager, I remember attending the church and seeing his name engraved on the outside of the building as one of the key organizers and leaders. As I reflect upon my grandparents, these memories remind me that I come from leaders and activists. My grandparents' work in the community reminds me that through leadership and spiritual faith I too can have a positive effect on my family and community. That is who I saw them be and that is how they trained me to be as well.

Dr. Janeé's Proud Family Moments

I don't know much about my family's history, but I have a great deal of pride stemming from the relationships with the people in my family now. While growing up, my aunts and uncles played a significant role in raising me. Some of them weren't much older than me, with the youngest being only 10 years old when I was born, but they still took responsibility for helping me and my sister out with everyday things like doing our hair, taking us shopping, or even just playing with us. On my mother's side, my aunts and uncles did not start out in life with much. My grandfather, their father, died when my youngest aunt was only 12 years old and my grandmother struggled with mental health issues for many years after that. Yet, in spite of all of the hardships they had to endure, each one of my aunts and uncles became adults with successful family lives and careers, having become business owners, administrators, tradesmen, lawyers, and executives. If my family had a theme song, it would be, "Started from the bottom, now we're here!" Each time I go home to visit or speak with them on the phone, I am reminded of just how far we have come, and I feel grateful to God, knowing that none of it would have been possible without Him.

Your Proud Family Moments

Now, it's your turn. In the space provided, please reflect on your proud family moments and what these moments mean for you. If it's hard to recall proud family moments, we encourage you to reflect on what proud family moments you would like to create for your current family. In essence, what legacy would you like to leave your family as you become your most confident self?

_____

_____

_____

_____

_____

_____

_____

_____

_____

_____

_____

_____

_____

_____

_____

_____

_____

Finally, take a moment to look back at what you wrote periodically and know that greatness is in your DNA!

Goals Toward Greatness

Has anyone ever told you that "If you fail to plan, you plan to fail?" This saying means that without clearly detailed goals, the hopes and dreams you have for your life will never come to fruition. Conversely, having clearly defined goals sets you on the path to achieving your aims in life, step by step as you complete the actions necessary to fulfill your dreams. Moreover, beyond helping you to accomplish your dreams, having goals also has a positive effect on your self-esteem because as you achieve your goals you grow in confidence, perseverance, and problem-solving ability—many of the qualities that reflect a healthy sense of self-esteem. Essentially, having goals helps you to be great.

Becoming your personal definition of greatness may be difficult but it is not impossible. However, a first step to achieving your greatness is learning how to create specific, tangible goals. Goals are the dreams and accomplishments you want to achieve in life. Clearly defining your goals and the actions needed to achieve your goals increases the chances of your dreams becoming reality.

A time-honored way of setting clearly defined goals is called the SMART goal method (Doran, 1981). SMART stands for specific, measurable, attainable, realistic, and timely. *Specific* means that you clearly articulate what you are going to do. *Measurable* means that you have a clear vision for what your goal will look like once it is accomplished. *Attainable* means that you have the tools necessary to carry out the goal, while *realistic* means that you are motivated to use those tools in a way that will actually allow you to meet the goal. Finally, *timely* means that you have a specific date by which you will accomplish the goal. An example of a SMART goal in the area of self-care, for example, might be: "I will identify and implement at least one new self-care activity per week over the next three months."

Anything is Possible

Once you have the skills necessary to identify clearly defined goals, anything is possible. In the space provided, let's take a moment and dream together. We want you to reflect on health, career, spiritual, and relationship goals you could set for yourself. If the sky was the limit, what goals would you like to achieve in these four domains? We'd like you to focus on goals you can achieve within the next one to three months. As you write these goals, be sure to be realistic. Setting unrealistic goals that you don't reach can actually have a negative effect on your self-esteem, so you want to be sure to avoid this. For example, an overall health goal might be to lose 50 pounds but realistically it might be more appropriate to state your goal as losing 12 pounds in the next three months. Again, the goal here is to set yourself up for success. Now, let's get started!

Health goal: _____

_____

Career goal: _____

_____

Relationship goal: _____

_____

Spiritual goal: _____

_____

Identify the Actions Needed to Get There

As we mentioned, setting goals is a first step to achieving greatness. The next step is identifying specific actions you should take in order to achieve your goal. In this next part of this activity, we would like you to reflect on actions you can take to achieve each one of your goals and write them down in the space provided. For example, if your goal is to lose 12 pounds, then maybe your action items will be to start working out two to three times a week and decrease consumption of specific unhealthy foods. We've provided some ideas for actions you might take toward your goals in each of the four domains. Take your time and think about it and when you're ready, write what you come up with.

Actions toward your health goal: _____

_____

_____

Health action tips: Start exercising two to three times a week, start a food journal or use an app to make sure you're getting in the right amount of nutrition, or get a primary care doctor if you don't have one.

Actions toward your career goal: _____

_____

_____

Career action tips: Find a mentor of your same racial background, join a professional organization, or work on developing your resume.

Actions toward your relationship goal: _____

_____

_____

Relationship action tips: Make your world bigger by joining a social club or group, reach out to family or friends that you have not connected with in a long time, or set boundaries with people in your personal life.

Actions toward your spiritual goal: _____

_____

_____

Spiritual action tips: Commit to reading a book that connects to your faith, find a place of worship, or commit to engaging in daily prayer.

Bonus: Writing your goals down helps you commit them to action, but it can also be beneficial to post your goals and action items somewhere in your home so that you are reminded of your commitment to achieve them. Try posting them on the bathroom mirror, your refrigerator, or anyplace that will keep them visible to you on a daily basis.

Visualize Your Greatness

There is a famous expression that says, "If you can see it, then you can be it." This expression means that if you can visualize yourself doing something, chances are you'll be able to do what you have visualized in real life. We chose to include an exercise on visualization in this workbook because the idea that we first need to see ourselves accomplishing our goals if we want to achieve them is not just wishful or positive thinking. Research actually shows that visualization of one's performance before a certain event can lead to positive feelings and beliefs, which in turn can positively affect one's real-life performance (Battistin, 2019). Recognizing this fact is especially important for Black people as it relates to racial healing and building self-esteem, as it could be argued that part of slavery entailed not only stripping people of their physical freedom, but it also stripped people of their ability to dream and reach their full potential. Therefore, in this activity, we focus on visualization as a method to free your ability to dream. First, let's take a closer look at visualization and how it works.

The Power of Visualization

In psychology, *visualization* can be defined as "the process of creating a visual image in one's mind or mentally rehearsing a planned movement in order to learn skills or enhance performance" (American Psychological Association, n.d. d). In recent years, this process has become extremely popular in the media and among motivational speakers in part due to celebrities and sports figures who have attributed much of their success to visualization. Basketball legend Kobe Bryant, for example, has been quoted as saying, "Losers visualize the penalties of failure. Winners visualize the rewards of success." Among the many people who have spoken publicly about the power of visualization in their lives, people like Oprah Winfrey, Beyoncé, Dwayne Wade, and Idris Elba, we believe this quote from Kobe Bryant is especially powerful because it emphasizes an important fact about visualization, which is that whatever you visualize, whether positive or negative, is likely to come in your life. As long as visualization is going to work one way or the other in your life, you might as well put it to work for your good.

There are many ways to practice visualization. Generally, visualization is an easy process that involves closing your eyes and mentally rehearsing what you hope to see become a reality in your life. According to licensed professional counselor, Wendy Boring-Bray (2021), this process can be accomplished in as little as five to ten minutes per day by simply following these steps:

1. Find a quiet place where you will not be disturbed.
2. Close your eyes and use your favorite breathing exercise to help you relax.
3. Think about the outcome or goal you want to achieve in your life. Visualize every detail of the outcome, including the steps it will take you to get there. **Pro tip:** Be sure to allow yourself to experience the feelings and emotions connected to achieving your goal.
4. Do this at least once a day, but preferably more.

(Boring-Bray, 2021, "What is Visualization")

Try it for Yourself

Beyond improved performance, visualization also has other benefits such as stress and anxiety reduction, as well as a more positive view of oneself (Boring-Bray, 2021). For example, among African American middle schoolers, visualization has been found to help students see the possibilities in their lives and to connect their current attitudes and behaviors with their hopes and dreams (Gibson, 1998). While the steps to visualization are not difficult, becoming good at visualization and other meditative exercises takes time and practice. This is because it's normal for our minds to wander and become distracted. Accordingly, one of the easiest ways to start out with visualization is through guided visualization. *Guided visualization* is a type of visualization wherein you listen to recordings that are designed to help you relax or engage in positive changes or actions. Because we think it's important for you to visualize yourself accomplishing your unique, individual goals, we recommend that you make and use your own guided visualizations using your smartphone or some other recording device. In what follows, you will find a generic example of a guided visualization script. After reading this example, we encourage you to write and record your own script. It may be helpful to refer to a specific goal or goals in order to make your script as effective as possible.

Example Visualization Script

I am practicing visualization today because I believe in myself and my dreams. I want to accomplish my goals and I know that if I can see it, I can be it.
To start, get in a comfortable position, maybe laying on the bed or the sofa. Then, close your eyes. Next, see yourself accomplishing each step of your goal and how you feel as you accomplish each step.
I see myself as confident and walking in that confidence as I achieve my goals.
Now that you have created this picture in your mind, allow yourself the next three minutes to just sit and feel, enjoy, and express gratitude for what will be manifested in your life.

Your Visualization Script

_____

_____

_____

_____

_____

_____

_____

_____

_____

_____

_____

_____

Reflection Questions

1. What was it like seeing yourself confident and having achieved your goals?

   _____

   _____

   _____

2. What emotions do you experience when you visualize yourself as successful and achieving goals?

   _____

   _____

   _____

3. What impact did this visualization have on your self-esteem? What could make it more effective?

   _____

   _____

   _____

Create Your Catchphrase

Whew! You've done a lot of hard work in this part of the workbook! The final self-esteem activity is a short mindfulness exercise designed to reinforce the role of positive self-talk in creating a healthy view of yourself. In this activity, you'll create a saying you can use in order to boost yourself when times get tough or in the face of adversity. Let's get started by using our imagination to guess what two of our ancestors, Harriet Tubman and Rosa Parks, may have used as their catchphrases.

Now, we would like for you to take a moment and create your own catchphrase bubbles. What can you say to yourself when faced with adversity or when you feel mistreated, especially when you are mistreated due to your racial identity? Place these messages in the blank bubbles.

Copyright material from Janeé M. Steele and Charmeka S. Newton (2023) *Black Lives Are Beautiful*, Routledge

Bonus: Now that you've created your own catchphrase, you can take this idea even further by writing affirmations to additionally bolster and improve your self-esteem. Affirmation cards are thoughtful first-person statements that encourage positive thinking and good self-esteem. These cards can help you create new narratives about yourself and challenge internalized racism and self-hate. You can write them using index cards or on plain paper. As you work to write your affirmation cards remember that they should be written using your own language, as this will allow you to connect more with the statements. Additionally, if you are religious or spiritual, the use of scripture can be instrumental for developing these cards. Here are some example affirmations:

- ❏ "I rise. I grind. I shine."
- ❏ "I am good enough. Period."
- ❏ "What we won't do is give up."
- ❏ "I come from survivors. I am a survivor."

PART 3

Tools to Promote Resilience

DOI: 10.4324/9781003221357-21

According to psychologists, *resilience* can be defined as the process of adapting well in the face of adversity, trauma, tragedy, threats, or significant sources of stress (Wald et al., 2006). Illustration of this term can be seen in the childhood story, *The Little Engine that Could.* In this folktale, the Little Blue Engine, a small train, was tasked with carrying cars full of good things for boys and girls up a steep mountain. Because of her size, Little Blue Engine struggled. After several other more powerful locomotives refused to help Little Blue Engine, she resolved within herself to make it up the mountain by herself, all the while repeating the famous line, "I think I can. I think I can. I think I can."

Little Blue Engine believed in herself, showing a great deal of resilience as she made her way up the mountain, ultimately delivering her supplies. Similar to Little Blue Engine, we as the Black community have been required to have that same undefeated spirit as the little locomotive. While Black people are not the only racial group to endure generational atrocities in the United States, our story is unique given the continued devastation that occurs in our community due to racism. We have had many mountains to climb, as we were forcibly brought to the United Stated and then systematically dehumanized by those in positions of power, even being legally denied civil and human rights. Yet, even in the face of all this we as a people survive and achieve greatness. We as a people have exemplified resilience. You can draw on this resilience as you continue to strive toward optimal development and racial healing.

Why is Resilience Important?

Due to racism, Black people experience challenges that can be overwhelming and difficult to navigate. For example, African Americans are more likely to experience disparate social and developmental outcomes including poverty, violent neighborhoods, and higher mortality rates due to disease, necessitating a need for strategies that facilitate an ability to overcome difficulties, also known as resilience (Brown, 2008). Research suggests that resilience is highly interconnected with positive racial socialization and social supports (Brown, 2008). Social supports within the Black community include immediate and extended family, the community, Black churches, and fictive kin, or individuals who are not biologically related to the family but have a role in childrearing (Brown, 2008). It is believed that through developing a sense of resilience, particularly in connection with positive racial socialization, Black people can counteract some of the negativity that comes from racism and oppression. Accordingly, having pride in cultural heritage, learning how to maintain a positive outlook, having a firm support system, and taking proactive steps to improve your life can go a long way toward mastering life's challenges without succumbing to the psychological stress these challenges entail.

Black People Do Go to Therapy

Within the Black community, there has been some stigma associated with going to therapy. Recently, however, people within the community, ranging from celebrities to average citizens, have been making efforts to reduce this stigma. Accordingly, a number of referral sources aimed toward connecting Black clients with Black therapists have been developed. In the following list, you will see some of these sources. If you do not already have a therapist, we recommend that you contact one of these sources and connect with one today. Everyone can benefit from therapy.

- ❏ Therapy for Black Girls (https://therapyforblackgirls.com/)
- ❏ Therapy for Black Men (https://therapyforblackmen.org/)
- ❏ Black Therapists Rock (www.blacktherapistsrock.om/)

How Do We Develop Resilience?

In essence, the challenges that we face as Black people require a certain level of tenacity in order to thrive within our society. In taking a closer look at resilience, it can be helpful to explore it across three levels: (1) individual, (2) family, and (3) community (Brown, 2008). At the *individual level*, you can develop resilience by learning cognitive strategies such as positive self-talk, which teaches you to see yourself as capable rather than as a helpless or hopeless victim. Another way to build resilience through your cognitive abilities is by participating in formal counseling such as cognitive behavior therapy. Through the use of cognitive behavior therapy, therapists help their clients learn ways to identify and reframe negative or maladaptive messages that may be given to them due to race-based experiences. If you do not currently have a therapist, you can try one of the many new referral sources designed to connect Black clients with Black therapists.

Another way to build resilience at the individual level is by focusing on self-efficacy. As we mentioned in our discussion on self-esteem, individuals who have self-efficacy believe they are able to solve problems. This is especially important as it relates to navigating experiences with racism, as challenging prejudice and discrimination can have a positive effect on one's overall psychological functioning. Similarly, resilience can also be built through self-regulation skills. People who are self-regulated are better able to manage their emotions and are less likely to feel overwhelmed, frustrated, or aggressive. Examples of self-regulation skills beyond positive self-talk include art, walking, journaling, eating healthy, and getting plenty of sleep. Connecting with your faith through strategies such as praise and worship, music, sermons, or even scriptures is yet another skill to build resilience. Overall, people who use these skills to manage their feelings still feel sadness, loss, or other emotions, but they're able to find healthy ways to cope. Moreover, people who use these skills also tend to experience better outcomes than people who rely on other, more harmful or maladaptive regulation strategies such as overeating, drinking, or perhaps smoking.

On a *family level*, you can build resilience by identifying the people you can rely on for support. Who are the people in your life, either biologically or in terms of chosen family, that you can count on to provide a safe haven when the world doesn't feel so safe? Generating this list of people before you experience problems can remind you of the resources and support you have and help you to feel calmer when you do encounter difficulties.

Lastly, on the *community level*, you can build strength and resilience by engaging with community-based organizations that support and affirm your racial identity. Schools, community centers, places of worship, and non-profit organizations are all groups you can become a part of in order to learn more about the issues affecting you and how to change them. For people affected by systemic oppression, this is especially powerful, as research indicates that spending time engaged in activities that focus on empowerment or serving others can teach you to focus on your cultural strengths and increase your feelings of personal control (Brown, 2008).

What We Are Not Saying

In an award acceptance speech, actor Jesse Williams was once quoted as saying in reference to Black people, "The thing is that just because we're magic doesn't mean we're not real" (Rankin, 2016). Williams was met with a standing ovation to this statement, as he rightfully recognized that while Black people have extraordinary cultural strengths, these strengths should not be used to negate the fact that Black people are still tangibly affected by the societal ills that intrude on their lives (Anderson, 2019).

Along those lines, while resilience is important, we want to acknowledge that this term can be conceptualized in a way that can be damaging or demeaning. The fact that Black people can be resilient does not mean that others, especially those in positions of power, should ignore the changes that need to occur within the environment in order to reduce racial discrimination and oppression. Being strong and resilient has consequences. While individuals may adapt and positively cope with the pain they have experienced as a result of racism, over time, this process can wear on one's emotional, psychological, spiritual, and physical health. As we've previously discussed, dealing with reoccurring racial discrimination has been directly linked to symptoms of anxiety and depression (Banks et al., 2006). While being resilient by definition means that a person is able to face challenges without significant harm to their mental health, no one is able to do this forever. Because racism is an ongoing problem in our society, we recognize that telling individuals to be resilient without also challenging the system is irresponsible (Anderson, 2019). Therefore, we want to be sure to emphasize the idea that while resilience can be used to protect us from racialized trauma, it does not replace the long-term need to eradicate racism. Accordingly, efforts are taken in this part to contextualize the discussion of resilience to reflect the importance of drawing on personal strengths without sacrificing one's mental health, and while also holding those in positions of power accountable.

What's to Come

In this part of the workbook, you will explore various aspects of resilience through the lens of racial socialization and social supports to encourage you to use your faith, ancestor background, inner resources, and external supports to find the strength needed to bounce back from obstacles you face. So, are you ready to do some more work? We hope the answer is yes because "We know you can. We know you can. We know you can."

Metaphor of Life

As we attempt to build resilience as a source of protection from the events of our lives that may have caused some level of brokenness, we must first engage in introspection. *Introspection* is our ability to examine our emotional and mental states. In essence, it is difficult to build resilience without gaining insight into how we as Black people interact with and build meaning concerning the world around us. In fact, research has supported the idea that resilience is not as much of an individual construct as it is a quality of the environment we create around us to facilitate growth (Ungar, 2013).

Use of metaphors can provide us with the insight needed to understand how we as individuals act with our environments to build resilience. In what follows we use the analogy of a plane to paint a picture of how different aspects of ourselves can help us be resilient. Similar to life, plane rides can be wonderful, rocky, smooth, exciting, and terrifying all at the same time. There are many factors that go into the operation of a plane and the experience of the ride. As you read about each of the seven key components that impact the plane experience, think about the various parts of yourself and your life that similarly contribute to your sense of resilience and how you deal with the turbulence of life.

1. **Power plant.** The power plant is the part of the plane that propels it forward and keeps it moving in the right direction. For the purpose of this metaphor, our power plant is our brain and the thoughts that we

form. The extent to which we are resilient and able to propel ourselves forward starts with our mindset and what we are thinking.

2. **Fuselage.** The fuselage is the cabin of the plane, the place where the people are housed. Our fuselage consists of who is "riding with us," "who has our back," or more specifically stated, who is supporting or helping us. Having people who are reliable and regularly show up in our lives can give us a sense of psychological fortitude because we know that we are not alone. Having people can also help us to have a more pleasant life.

3. **Empennage.** The empennage is the tail of the plane. It creates stability for the plane ride. In our own life, this consists of the things that keep us healthy like positive coping skills and stable relationships.

4. **Wings.** The wings of the plane are responsible for lifting up the plane while in the air. We can look at our wings as the things that lift us up, such as our spiritual faith or belief in a higher power, the use of affirmations, or surrounding ourselves with other sources of inspiration.

5. **Landing gear.** The landing gear allows the plane to land and stay grounded. You can view this part of your life as the things that successfully ground and center us, such as gratitude, compassion, kindness, and acceptance.

6. **Turbulence.** Turbulence occurs on an airplane ride as a result of wind currents that push or pull the airplane. In life, we are often met with turbulence in the form of uncontrollable life circumstances that may happen around us that create a rocky or unsettling experience. Though uncomfortable, this is a normal part of the ride.

7. **Air traffic control.** Finally, air traffic control is the external safety precaution pilots have to help guide and keep the plane safe. In our lives, these precautions may be trusted elders, counselors, advisors, spiritual leaders, or the Creator. Whoever you look to for guidance, these people help to keep us on track and warn us when there are potential dangers in the area.

In order for us to have a smooth ride on the airplane of life, there must be a balance between all the key components of the plane. For example, if the engine is not running smoothly, we can experience a rather jerky or challenging ride. Paying ample attention to each of the different elements can serve as a measure to protect our wellbeing. Conversely, ignoring the things that go on around us can make our ride unpleasant. The following reflection questions will help you to ensure that the components of your airplane are running smoothly and your ability to be resilient remains intact.

Reflection Questions

1. What life challenge are you currently facing? Write them down in the space provided.

   _____

   _____

   _____

2. Now, let's work with your "power plant" (i.e., your thoughts). What negative thoughts do you have about the challenges you are currently facing?

   _____

   _____

   _____

3. Next, let's identify some replacement thoughts. Replacement thoughts might be "I am capable of handling this task" or "I need to extend some grace to myself." What thoughts can you tell yourself to replace the negative thinking you have about your challenges?

   _____

   _____

   _____

4. Now that we have our thoughts in order, let's look at your fuselage system and see who is "rolling with us." Identify the people that can provide support, resources, or knowledge as you deal with you challenges. List them here.

   _____

   _____

   _____

5. How can you ask for the help that you need from the people that are "rolling with you?"

    _____

    _____

    _____

6. Is anybody rolling with you that may need to exit the plane? Is there anyone lessening your ability to be resilient?

    _____

    _____

    _____

7. How might you set some boundaries with this person that should not be rolling with you? Some ideas on how to set boundaries might be saying "no," putting a time limit on your interaction with the person, or having an honest conversation with the person about the need to set boundaries in the relationship.

    _____

    _____

    _____

8. Next, let's look at how your empennage system is running. What healthy coping skills are you using as you face this challenge? For example, are you exercising, getting enough sleep, eating a healthy diet? In the space provided here, identify the coping skills that can help you provide stability as you seek to be resilient. Perhaps looking at what has helped you before can be useful.

    _____

    _____

    _____

9. Next, let's check your landing gear. What grounding exercises can you do to create a sense of resilience? Listed here are some examples. Circle ones you might try.
   - Deep breathing by breathing the air in through your nose and breathing it our slowly through your mouth.
   - Go for a mindfulness walk and appreciating everything you see on the walk.
   - Feel your feet on the floor by sitting in a comfortable position and just feeling your feet on the floor for 1 minute.
   - Do a guided relaxation using the Calm or Headspace app.
   - Create your own: _____

10. How about we check your wings now. What are some things that will uplift you and keep you feeling safe during this challenging time?

    _____

    _____

    _____

11. Let's look at the turbulence around you. What are things that knock you, shake you, or create noise and stop you from enjoying the ride?

    _____

    _____

    _____

12. How might you use your air traffic control to reduce some of the noise described in the previous question?

    _____

    _____

    _____

Standing on the Shoulders of Giants

As Black people, we stand on the shoulders of giants. This means that the life and liberty we have now was made possible by the sacrifices of our ancestors, mentors, and others who fought and sometimes died for the rights we enjoy today. Many of these individuals never knew us or our family members personally, but they believed that we as a people deserved to be free and to follow in the sentiment of Dr. Martin Luther King Jr.'s famous speech and not be judged by our skin color.

Acknowledging the memories of those on whose shoulders we stand is a powerful way to enhance our sense of resilience, especially within the context of the relationship between resilience and racial socialization. Recall that broadly, *racial socialization* refers to the extent to which you feel pride in your race or ethnicity. People with stronger racial socialization tend to have a greater sense of resilience and are better equipped to handle the psychological fallout of racial prejudice, discrimination, or harassment. For example, according to research conducted by Brown and Tylka (2011), African Americans who report receiving more positive racial socialization messages from their parents or caregivers as teenagers have greater resilience when confronted with racial discrimination. Moreover, racial socialization messages that emphasize one's cultural legacy have an especially significant impact on resilience in the face of discrimination, suggesting that messages that focus on one's cultural legacy "may be more helpful than messages that simply instruct children to be proud of being an African American without providing a foundation for why they should be proud (e.g., the history and legacy of civil rights)" (Brown & Tylka, 2011, p. 276).

Focusing on Your Cultural Legacy

Given the research findings regarding the role of cultural legacy in resilience and its protection against racial discrimination (Brown & Tylka, 2011), we think it can be helpful to identify aspects of your cultural legacy you can focus on as you encounter racial hostility in your own environment. Next we provide an excerpt from the autobiography of Nelson Mandela (1995), the first Black president of South Africa and one of the key figures responsible for ending apartheid in the country, as an example of an ancestor from whose strength we can derive a sense of resilience. After reading the excerpt, respond to the subsequent reflection questions to explore examples you believe are important to your own cultural legacy. As you do, be sure to focus on examples that illustrate the type of strength necessary to persevere in the face of racial prejudice, harassment, or discrimination. These examples can come from the entirety of Black history or your personal family. Feel free to write about any event or person that makes you feel proud to be Black and proves that it's possible to cope with difficulties in life.

Ancestor Nelson Mandela

It was during those long and lonely years that my hunger for the freedom of my own people became a hunger for the freedom of all people, white and black. I knew as well as I knew anything that the oppressor must be liberated just as surely as the oppressed. A man who takes away another man's freedom is a prisoner of hatred, he is locked behind the bars of prejudice and narrow-mindedness. I am not truly free if I am taking away someone else's freedom, just as surely as I am not free when my freedom is taken from me. The oppressed and the oppressor alike are robbed of their humanity.

When I walked out of prison that was my mission, to liberate the oppressed and the oppressor both. Some say that has now been achieved. But I know that that is not the case. The truth is that we are not yet free; we have merely achieved the freedom to be free, the right not to be oppressed. We have not taken the final step of our journey, but the first step on a longer and even more difficult road. For to be free is not merely to cast off one's chains, but to live in a way that respects and enhances the freedom of others. The true test of our devotion to freedom is just beginning.

(Mandela, 1995, pp. 624–625)

Reflection Questions

1. Who are some of the giants upon whose shoulders you stand?

   _____

   _____

   _____

2. How have they made your life better?

   _____

   _____

   _____

3. How can you use their resilience as a model of how you can be resilient?

   _____

   _____

   _____

4. What final lessons can you observe from them in terms of bouncing back and overcoming?

   _____

   _____

   _____

Challenge: As you move forward with building your resilience, remembering those who came before you and drawing on their strength is important. It might even be helpful to find pictures of your giants or symbols that represent them in order to make a collage you can keep in a visible place to remind you of the strength of those who have gone before you.

Your Family Story

There is a popular show on National Public Radio called Story Corps. On this show, regular people tell fascinating stories about their lives—stories about love and hate, heartache and redemption, triumph and disappointment. While we generally enjoy listening to these stories, at times they elicit feelings of sadness, especially when the stories consist of family or immigration histories. Many people with European ancestry can trace their family history back to its origins. Unfortunately, due to slavery, many African Americans cannot trace their family history back to their country of origin. As a result of the latter situation, our family histories are often limited, and our ancestral knowledge can be fragmented.

In spite of limitations in our ability to trace our family history, knowing what you can determine about your personal history is beneficial to the development of resilience. As we've emphasized, knowing where you come from and the history of your people can provide you with strength and cultural pride, which leads to greater personal insight and coping (Brown, 2008). Moreover, it can give you hope for the future as you realize that many of the goals and dreams your ancestors had for their descendants came true. Evidence of this can be seen on another show called Finding Your Roots. On this show, which airs on Public Broadcasting Service, Dr. Henry Louis Gates, Jr. digs into the ancestral past of politicians, celebrities, and other well-known individuals, discovering the stories of the individuals who laid the foundation for their success. While the interviews and revelations are always poignant, the episodes featuring African Americans are always the most touching, as the information Dr. Gates and his team is able to uncover about the guest's family histories represents knowledge that is typically lost to many Black people.

In this final exercise focused on heritage, you get to create your own version of Finding Your Roots by finding the oldest living member of your family and engaging them in an interview. This task can be done in one setting, over several weeks, or across several months. In the following list there are some sample questions that you might ask during the interview. With your relative's permission, you may want to audio or video record the interview, as there may be a wealth of information that can be passed down for generations to come.

- ❏ When and where were you born?
- ❏ How did our family come to live there?
- ❏ What is your earliest childhood memory?
- ❏ How did our family deal with hard times and setbacks?
- ❏ Do you remember experiencing any discrimination or prejudice? If so, how did you handle it?
- ❏ What family traditions do you remember?
- ❏ What are some of the stories that have come down to you about your parents, grandparents, or maybe even more distant ancestors?
- ❏ What things bring you a sense of pride concerning our family heritage?
- ❏ What are struggles you have had to overcome as a person of color? How have you overcome those struggles?
- ❏ Of all the things you learned from your parents, what do you feel was the most valuable?

Bonus: Once you have completed the interview take some time and reflect upon the information shared. The following reflection questions might help.

Reflection Questions

1. What will you do with what you have learned?

   _____

   _____

   _____

   _____

   _____

   _____

   _____

2. If you noticed struggles or adversities within what was shared how will you use that information to motivate or inspire yourself?

   _____

   _____

   _____

   _____

   _____

   _____

   _____

3. How can you take the information that was shared and pass it down to others in your family?

   _____

   _____

   _____

   _____

   _____

   _____

   _____

   _____

You're a Survivor

In the previous activity, you identified ancestors that exemplify the type of strength and cultural pride we can draw from as our own source of resilience. As you think about these individuals, it is important to note that you too have their "survivor" spirit. Whether the ancestors you identified survived the transatlantic crossing during slavery, worked in the hot cotton-fields, fought for our civil rights, or were the first in their schools or professions, the fact of the matter is that they persevered and their lineage is in your DNA. You are a survivor.

Seeing the strength of your ancestors in yourself is an important aspect of resilience. This is because your strength provides you with evidence that you are resilient. Essentially, the more resilience you have, the more strengths and competencies you are able to engage in when confronted with difficulties. According to the research, the personal strengths associated with resilience tend to lie in four areas: (1) social competence, (2) problem solving, (3) autonomy, and (4) a sense of purpose (Benard, 2004). Acknowledging your strengths in these areas can be a beneficial intervention because it leaves you feeling empowered and motivated (Tedeschi & Kilmer, 2005). Moreover, it gives you a more balanced view of yourself, which is especially important if you tend to be overly critical or harsh toward yourself. Therefore, this activity focuses on helping you to acknowledge and assess your strengths with an overall goal of highlighting the qualities you have within yourself for coping and handling life's difficulties.

Assessing Your Strengths

Now that you have a greater understanding of the connection between your strengths and resilience, let's take a moment and identify the positive attributes you possess. Read the following list and circle any of the attributes that relate to you.

Action oriented	Empathic	Persistent
Adaptable	Hardworking	Problem solver
Brave	Heroic	Purposeful
Brilliant	Hopeful	Rational
Calm	Humorous	Resourceful
Charismatic	Insightful	Respectful
Committed	Invaluable	Responsible
Competent	Logical	Self-aware
Confident	Love of learning	Self-controlled
Cooperative	Mentally tough	Self-directed
Creative	Motivated	Skillful
Critical thinker	Nurturing	Smart
Curious	Optimism	Sociable
Decisive	Orderly	Strong
Dedicated	Passionate	Wise
Determined	Patience	

Reflection Questions

1. What feelings came up for you as you read the list and thought about your personal strengths? Where do you think these come from?

   _____

   _____

   _____

   _____

   _____

   _____

2. As you look at the strengths you circled, recall that strengths connected to resilience tend to reflect social competence, problem solving, autonomy, and sense of purpose. What categories do your strengths belong to?

   _____

   _____

   _____

   _____

   _____

   _____

3. Continuing to think about the categories of resilience strengths (i.e., social competence, problem solving, autonomy, and sense of purpose), how can you do more of what you are good at? How can you manage your areas for growth?

   _____

   _____

   _____

   _____

   _____

   _____

"I Am" Statements

Let's not stop there with the assessment of your strengths. Acknowledging your positive attributes is a good way to emphasize your strengths, which leads to a fortified sense of resilience; however, using "I am" statements to express these attributes can be an even more powerful way of imprinting your resilience on your psyche. Take the attributes you circled previously and create "I am" statements you can use to remind yourself of the things that help you bounce back. An example of an "I am" statement would be, "I am resourceful." When you are finished, read each one of your "I am" statements out loud, remembering that there is power in what we speak.

_____

_____

_____

_____

_____

_____

_____

_____

_____

_____

_____

_____

_____

_____

_____

_____

_____

Rewrite the Narrative

Many of the ideas we have concerning ourselves and others come from the stories told about the events that occur in our lives. *Narrative therapy*, which is a form of therapy focused on reinterpreting events into more life-enhancing stories, can be particularly useful in contributing to resilience by countering the negative messages we receive about Black people (American Psychological Association, n.d. a). As discussed previously, individuals often internalize negative messages about their racial group. These messages often lead to feelings of helplessness. Rewriting these narratives can help you reclaim your sense of power through increased cultural pride. Dr. Martin Luther King, Jr. expresses this very idea in the following quote taken from one of his speeches:

> Somebody told a lie one day. They couched it in language. They made everything black ugly and evil. Look in your dictionaries and see the synonyms of the word black. It's always something degrading and low and sinister. Look at the word white, it's always something pure, high, and clean. Well, I want to get the language right tonight. I want to get the language so right that everyone here will cry out, 'Yes, I'm Black, I'm proud of it. I'm Black and I'm beautiful!'
>
> (Savali, 2014, para. 6)

In this quote, Dr. King acknowledges that the prevailing discourse over time has portrayed the word black, and by proxy Black people, as low and threatening, while things associated with the word white, and by proxy White people, have been portrayed as pure and superior. However, Dr. King also recognized that we could challenge prevailing discourses and their impact on how we see ourselves as Black people by being intentional about the language we use to tell the story of who we are and where we come from. In this activity, you will begin this process of countering false or negative messages that have been promulgated about Black people as a community and about you as an individual. To do so, respond to the following questions. Once you have answered each question, return to your responses on a daily basis, remembering that it takes time and intentionality to change the negative beliefs we have been exposed or socialized into.

1. Take a moment and think about the lies that are told about Black people. These might be lies that you see in the media or hear in your environment. Jot down some of those lies in the space provided.

   _____

   _____

   _____

2. Next, rewrite the lies. What do you know to be true about your people, your community?

   _____

   _____

   _____

3. Now, write down the lies that have been said about you specifically as a person of color. Maybe it's that you're not smart enough or capable. List those lies here.

   _____

   _____

   _____

4. Finally, give it some truth. Write down what you know to be true about yourself. You may want to revisit some of your "I am" statement from the previous activity.

   _____

   _____

   _____

Self-Compassion

In Part 1, we discussed self-compassion as a tool for racial healing. *Self-compassion* can be defined as the ongoing practice of relating to yourself kindly and fairly (Whitlock et al., 2021). It entails extending yourself grace and engaging in positive self-talk. It also entails treating yourself as you would treat a friend who is in distress, especially during times when you are confronted with stress and unexpected challenges (Whitlock et al., 2021). Accordingly, some researchers believe that self-compassion is one of the most powerful sources of resilience we have (Neff, 2016). Therefore, this activity focuses on ways you can integrate self-compassion into your life as part of an overall strategy for increasing inner resources associated with resilience.

Components of Self-Compassion

According to Whitlock et al. (2021), self-compassion consists of three specific elements: (1) mindfulness, (2) self-kindness, and (3) common humanity. *Mindfulness* refers to being aware of the physical, emotional, or mental pain of the moment. *Self-kindness* refers to the importance of considering your own needs. *Common humanity* refers to recognizing that obstacles, difficulties, and hardships are common to all members of humanity. These three elements of self-compassion contribute to resilience by increasing wellbeing and resistance to stress and trauma. They additionally foster resilience by encouraging individuals to develop a mindset that is focused on learning from difficult experiences rather than criticizing or judging oneself harshly for these experiences. This is perhaps the most beneficial aspect of self-compassion, as this mindset prepares us for future challenges.

While mindfulness approaches such as self-compassion have been around for a long time, some individuals have negative views of these strategies, believing them to be fads or wishful thinking. What negative impressions do you have of self-compassion? Write these impressions in the space provided. Then, write down potential benefits to being more open toward self-compassion.

_____

_____

_____

_____

_____

_____

_____

_____

Exercising Self-Compassion

Let's practice working with our thoughts (see the following figure, Uncompassionate Thoughts). In the Uncompassionate Thoughts triangle let's work with a thought that you often think about yourself that is not so kind. In the thought box write the thought. Then, in the feeling box write how it makes you feel when thinking that thought. Make sure you use feeling words like *sad*, *mad*, or *disappointed*. Lastly, in the behavior box, write down how this thought causes you to behave, or in other words, the actions you engage in when thinking this thought and having these feelings.

Example thought: "I should be doing better in life."

Example feeling(s): Sad, hopeless, angry, frustrated, and helpless.

Example behavior(s): Give up trying and isolate myself.

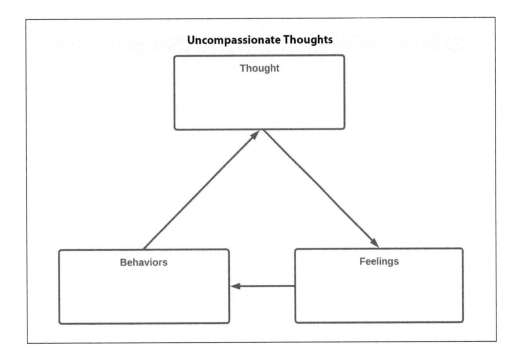

Now, let's work on extending some grace and kindness to yourself. In this next triangle, think of a more compassionate thought to replace the first thought and complete the triangle using that thought.

Example of compassionate thought: "I need to take it a day at a time and my hard work and dedication will pay off."

Example feeling(s): Hopeful, some mild excitement, and happiness.

Example behavior(s): Continue working toward my goals and look for ways to gain the success I desire.

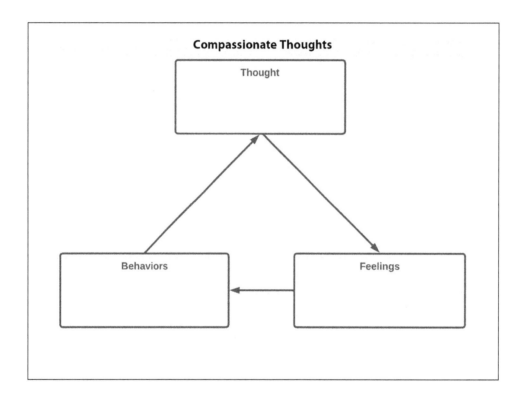

Self-Compassion Daily Habits

In addition to working with our thoughts and giving ourselves compassion, we can also engage in actions that create balance and help us to be resilient. For each day of the week, pick one thing you can do to show kindness toward yourself. Maybe it's taking a long relaxing bath, doing some deep breathing, preparing yourself a healthy meal, or going for a walk/run. Whatever you pick, be intentional in doing something every day and write it in the following chart. After you complete the activity, be sure to also reflect on the activity and rate your mood using the simple smiley face rating scale also in the chart.

TABLE 23.1

Seven Days of Self-Compassion

Activity	Rating
Sunday	😟 😕 😐 🙂 😊
Monday	😟 😕 😐 🙂 😊
Tuesday	😟 😕 😐 🙂 😊
Wednesday	😟 😕 😐 🙂 😊
Thursday	😟 😕 😐 🙂 😊
Friday	😟 😕 😐 🙂 😊
Saturday	😟 😕 😐 🙂 😊

What's Next? Once you have completed your seven days of self-compassion, go back and look at the things that brought you the most happiness. These activities might be positive coping skills for you and things you should continue doing.

Purpose and Resilience

Purpose can be defined as the reason(s) for our existence. It can also be looked at as the things we are passionate about or the things we aspire to accomplish. Sometimes purpose is connected with our spiritual faith, career goals, family, or even the work we do in our community. Regardless of the area of focus, having a sense of purpose is essential for building resilience and persevering when faced with obstacles. Moreover, research has shown that if we have purpose, we are more likely to live longer, have better health, make better choices and emerge from life's obstacles stronger than before (Benard, 2004). Therefore, this activity is designed to help you explore what you currently define as your purpose with the hopes of providing some of the motivation needed to maintain resilience throughout your life.

Identifying Your Purpose

In the blank tree branch bubbles, write what you believe your purposes in life are.

Reflection Questions
1. How did it feel writing about your purpose? Did you struggle? What was clear about your purpose(s)?

If you struggled with defining your purpose, or even if you want to go deeper and discover other life purposes, here are some tips that might help:

❏ **Look at what breaks your heart.** Self-discovery is crucial for discovering your purpose. Asking yourself questions like, "What makes me sad when I see it occur?" "What really gets me excited or motivated?" "What am I passionate about?" or "Is there a problem I always wanted to solve?" can provide important clues to your purpose in life.

❏ **Help others.** When we go outside of ourselves and help others, we often learn about ourselves. For example, we may learn new skills or characteristics that we did not know we possessed. Whether you volunteer with a local non-profit or simply support a friend in their time of need, providing volunteer service can help you to gain a sense of purpose, connect with others, and make an impact, leading to discovery of your purpose.

❏ **Look for new experiences.** We never grow while stuck in our comfort zone. The more we move outside of what we are comfortable with, the more we can find purpose and meaning in life. Looking for new experience like starting a new craft, beginning a new educational experience, or connecting with a new group of people can help. Through new experiences we can engage in self-discovery and find purpose.

❏ **Set a goal and move toward it.** Developing realistic goals and doing something regularly to achieve your goals can help clarify your purpose. Ask yourself "What's one task I can do today to accomplish my goal?" In setting out to accomplish this task, try using the "15-minute rule" where you set a timer for 15 minutes to work on your goal so that you at least get something done toward your aim. For example, if one of your life purposes is to start your own business, for 15 minutes a day do something that will help you develop your business plan. If after working for that 15 minutes you still feel motivated, set the timer for another 15 minutes and continue working.

Manifesting Your Purpose

In the Racial Healing section of this workbook (pp. 21–68), we talked about the power of visualization in achieving your goals. As a refresher, *visualization* can be defined as "the process of creating a visual image in one's mind or mentally rehearsing a planned movement in order to learn skills or enhance performance" (American Psychological Association, n.d. d). In this activity, you will continue to explore how purpose might be used as a motivation for resilience, this time using visualization to help you imagine fully living in your purpose.

Step one: Set a timer for three minutes, close your eyes, and envision yourself living out your purpose. For a moment, imagine that you wake up tomorrow and you are fully living out your purpose. Maybe you own the business that you've been working on or perhaps you are living out your spiritual faith and sharing it with others. As you imagine this scenario, picture yourself acting "as if" everything associated with your purpose was a reality. "Acting as if" is an important strategy because when we visualize positive actions, our brain is stimulated in a way that is nearly identical to actually being engaged in the real activity. So, if you want to be confident and successful, it helps to first envision and then adjust the things you do, say, and think to be totally in line with your purpose.

Step two: Reflect upon what you saw as you envisioned yourself living out this purpose.

1. As you visualized yourself living out your purpose, what did you see?

    _____

    _____

    _____

    _____

    _____

2. How did you feel during the visualization?

    _____

    _____

    _____

    _____

    _____

3. What do you remember thinking in this moment?

    _____

    _____

    _____

    _____

    _____

Step three: Identify what you are already doing that you can do more of and what you can start doing. Now that you've imagined what life would be like if you were acting as if you are truly walking out your life purpose, how can you do more of what you are already doing that is in line with your purpose and what do you need to do more of? Write it in the following space.

_____

_____

_____

_____

Using Fun to Enhance Resilience

As we end this part of the workbook, we thought it would be a good idea to interject another quick bit of fun. One of the ways we build resilience is by engaging activities that are just a bit above our comfort level. Games, whether they be board games, sports, or even dance, can be a great way to work outside of our comfort zones and enhance our ability to stick with difficult things while also having fun.

For this activity, you will identify one game to which you are new at or have struggled with in the past. Then, you will engage this game regularly over whatever amount of time seems appropriate to you—one week, over the summer, or during winter break, for example. As you engage in this game, take note of the negative thoughts you have about yourself, your ability to perform, or your ability to accomplish your goal. Write these thoughts down in the space provided in Table 26.1. Then, come up with a positive reframe for each negative thought you have. When your time period is up, write down what you learned about yourself and your ability to persist in the face of adversity.

TABLE 26.1

Game Time!

Game	Negative Thoughts	Positive Reframes	What I Learned About Myself

PART 4

Tools to Promote Empowerment

DOI: 10.4324/9781003221357-31

A sigh of relief. Tears of joy. Pangs of sadness. A renewed sense of hope. These were just some of the emotions a large part of Black America felt as the guilty verdict in the trial for the murder of George Floyd was read on April 20, 2021. Ebbs and flows of emotions when dealing with the legal system is something African Americans have experienced since the founding of this country. In fact, this variability of emotions has not only been experienced in America's legal system, but within its educational, mass media, and economic spaces as well. While it is clear that the root problem in these spaces as it relates to Black people is racism, racism in this context is often experienced as a sense of disempowerment. *Disempowerment* in its simplest sense refers to limitations to one's ability to exert control over their life. From a sociocultural point of view, disempowerment has been devasting for the Black community. As a result of disempowerment, Black people have experienced negative consequences in most of the areas that have the greatest impact on our quality of life, including economics, health, and education (Jagers et al., 2017). These negative consequences to economics, health, and education, in turn, have a negative impact on our emotional, mental, and psychological wellbeing. Therefore, as we as a people work toward personal and collective healing, it is important to look to becoming more empowered, focusing on the restoration that can take place when we reclaim our rights to life, liberty, and justice in all spheres of life. Accordingly, this part of the workbook explores ways to gain a sense of empowerment despite the marginalized status we experience in society.

What is Empowerment?

Empowerment is defined as a process through which individuals gain confidence in their ability to: (a) assert control over their lives and (b) take action to improve their situations (Gutiérrez, 1995). In order to fully understand this definition, it may be helpful to first explore the concept of disempowerment. To *disempower* someone means to cause a person or a group of people to be less likely than others to succeed, or to prevent a person or group of people from having power, authority, or influence (Britannica Dictionary, n.d.). In the United States, disempowerment through the forcible denial of personal choice and power over one's life was a reality for our ancestors, and it continues to be a reality for us now (Britannica Dictionary, n.d.). In fact, some actually argue that the knee to Mr. Floyd's neck was a metaphoric knee to the necks of all Black people, symbolic of White supremacist attitudes and practices that currently hold down and disempower Black America. In our contemporary time, examples of these practices include residential segregation, unfair lending practices and barriers to home ownership and wealth, environmental injustice,

TABLE P.4.1

Free Your Mind

Becoming empowered begins with developing an understanding of the mindsets that cause us to think negatively about ourselves, or worse, to act in ways that reinforce our oppression. Here, we have included a list of attitudes and behaviors that reflect some of these mindsets. As you read the list, consider the following questions: • Which attitudes and behaviors have you exhibited in your own life? • What experiences have influenced the development of these attitudes and behaviors in your life? • What can you do to modify these attitudes and behaviors? • How can you show yourself compassion as you engage in the process of modifying these attitudes and behaviors?	
Attitudes	
Inferiority	Believing, either consciously or unconsciously, in the supremacy of White culture. "Being Black is at times embarrassing or shameful."
Inadequacy	Believing, either consciously or unconsciously, that you personally are inferior unless you conform to White cultural norms. "I'm not good enough unless I adopt certain interests, communication styles, and standards of beauty."
Personal blame	Taking complete responsibility for failures or difficulties even when prejudice and discrimination are factors. "All of my difficulties in life are my own fault."
Powerlessness	Believing that you are more limited in your ability to create change than you actually are. "Things will always stay the same. Nothing I do matters."
Belief in a just world	Believing there must be just reasons for the inequalities among racial groups, such as low morals or inferior intellectual abilities. "Everyone gets what they deserve."
Behaviors	
Avoidance	Attempting to cope with feelings of shame, embarrassment, and alienation by distancing oneself from aspects of being Black, for example, concealing the neighborhood you are from or isolating yourself from individuals and social settings you think confirm negative stereotypes.
Conformity	Adjusting your speech, appearance, or behavior to be more like the dominant culture, ranging on a continuum from code-switching to overt stigmatization of Black cultural norms.
Overperformance	Overperforming in occupational, academic, or social settings to meet real or perceived expectations greater than those held for members of the dominant racial group.
Learned helplessness	Doing nothing when challenged by racism because you don't believe you have any control over what happens.

Adapted from Steele and Newton (2022).

biased policing and sentencing of people of color, voter suppression, inequitable funding of schools, and disparate access to healthcare and mental health services (Braveman et al., 2022). We experience empowerment when we gain an understanding of the impact these policies have on our lives and become willing to challenge these and other similar forms of oppression.

There are many ways to become empowered. Empowerment can occur across multiple levels (e.g., individual, organizational, and community levels) and within several domains (e.g., economic, political, psychological). As therapists, we typically begin with a focus on psychological empowerment as a means to facilitate healing from racial trauma. *Psychological empowerment* has been defined as "(a) possession of a critical awareness about the issues affecting his or her community, (b) comprehension of his or her sociopolitical context, and (c) possession of the ability to identify and mobilize resources in the African American community" (Livingston et al., 2017, p. 286). The changes in worldview that occurred during the Civil Rights era are perhaps some of the most vivid examples of psychological empowerment to occur within the Black community. During this time, Black people began to develop, or at least express, a greater understanding of the detrimental impact White supremacy has on how we see ourselves and each other. In popular culture, for example, this understanding was expressed in music, with songs like "A Change is Going to Come" by Sam Cooke; in fashion, with Afrocentric styles such as afros and African print clothing; in plays, such as "A Raisin in the Sun"; in poetry, such as Langston Hughes's "A Dream Deferred"; and of course, in the Black is Beautiful movement. These works of art are good representations of psychological empowerment because while they did not in themselves lead to reforms in the laws and policies that limited personal choice and power for Black people, they did help provide the inspiration and courage needed to motivate those who were willing to fight for change.

Critical Consciousness

The definitions we provided earlier for empowerment and psychological empowerment both emphasize a commitment to initiating change in one's social environment (Gutiérrez, 1995; Zimmerman, 1995). While the role of social change in empowerment is significant, it is important to note that individuals typically do not engage in social change actions until they have first gained an awareness of the ways in which they have been oppressed or marginalized (Prilleltensky & Gonick, 1996). Therefore, critical consciousness is viewed as a foundational aspect of empowerment. *Critical consciousness* is defined as "the capacity of oppressed or marginalized people to critically analyze their social and political conditions, endorsement of societal equality, and action to change perceived inequities" (Diemer et al., 2017, p. 461). According to Gutiérrez (1995), it consists of three primary elements: (1) group identification, (2) group consciousness, and (3) self and collective agency. *Group identification* refers to the extent to which you identify as sharing common experiences and concerns as members of your racial group, having a preference for your own group's culture and norms, and having feelings of a shared fate with members of your racial group. *Group consciousness* refers to the extent to which you understand that various racial groups have different levels of status and power in society. Finally, *self and collective efficacy* broadly refers to beliefs that one is capable of effecting desired changes in one's life.

In our experience as therapists, we've found that individuals recognize the need for racial healing at various levels of critical consciousness. However, those with more advanced levels of critical consciousness usually have greater awareness of the socioeconomic, political, cultural, and psychological factors that influence their lives and a stronger belief in their capacity to challenge these factors (Prilleltensky & Gonick, 1996, p. 139). As a result, these individuals also tend to have greater motivation to use their strengths and problem-solving skills to exact change in their environments, for example, confronting racism in their jobs, schools, or relationships. We have additionally observed that individuals with greater critical consciousness also tend to have a stronger sense of agency as it relates to community engagement and speaking out against broader societal issues such as police brutality, limited access to resources, and underrepresentation of people of color in community organizations.

One of our clients, Sonja, illustrates the relationship between critical consciousness and empowerment. Sonja initially began counseling due to difficulties with anxiety. During the time she was in therapy, the murders of George Floyd, Breonna Taylor, and Ahmaud Arbery occurred. With each death, Sonja became increasingly distressed. Her anxiety increased and she also began to experience a depressed mood. Prior to these events, Sonja was an avid consumer of books and podcasts focused on topics such as White supremacy, anti-racism, and social justice. The insights she gained from these books and podcasts gave her the conceptual understanding needed to explain why these events are allowed to occur in our country and helped her to find the language she needed to express her anger and frustration. Yet, while being able to vent her feelings and frustrations provided Sonja some emotional relief, she did not begin to experience improvements in her mood and anxiety until she also began to engage in activism such as participating in protests, Facebook groups, and local community groups. Sonja reported that by participating in these activities, she was able to feel closer to other members of the Black community, which provided a sense of safety and belonging and greater optimism. Essentially, Sonja felt empowered. This sense of empowerment, in turn, decreased her feelings of depression and anxiety. Moreover, Sonja also experienced other benefits as a result of her greater sense of empowerment, including increased openness about her sexual identity and greater willingness to also be a change agent on her job and in the various community organizations of which she was a member.

What is Your Vision?

We've found that over time and with the support of friends, family, community, and sometimes a therapist, several interventions can help individuals increase their critical consciousness and sense of empowerment. In this part, we've included activities, based on what we have seen, that are the best at promoting understanding of the internal and external factors that influence empowerment and a willingness to work toward social change. These activities focus on building your critical consciousness, self-determination, leadership skills, and sociopolitical engagement, as well as teaching you how to disarm and challenge racial bias and discrimination (Sue et al., 2019). However, recognizing that no change within oneself or the community can occur without first having a vision for the future, we believe that before engaging in the following activities, it is important that you first begin to develop a vision for yourself as it relates to empowerment. In what follows, we invite you to write or even draw a vision of what a more empowered you would look like. This vision can consist of new attitudes and behaviors you would like to see in yourself, or the goals you have for your family, community, or other important affiliations. After you've completed the activities, come back to this vision to add anything you may have discovered about yourself or your goals. Then, review this page periodically to check on your progress.

I Have A Dream

Rev. Dr. Martin Luther King, Jr. had a dream that his four children would one day live in a nation where they would not be judged by their skin color. This dream for the future motivated Dr. King to pursue his goals for civil and economic rights through all kinds of hardships, even to the point of death. What vision of the future motivates you? In the following space, write or draw a picture of your dream for a better tomorrow. Every so often, refer back to this dream, monitoring your progress and refining your vision as necessary.

Music for Your Soul

Let's have a little fun. Complete the following song title:

"Say it loud, I'm Black and _____." —James Brown

Music has long been a part of Black culture. Starting in Africa and continuing in the Americas after the Transatlantic Slave Trade, music has served as a way to pass down information, to connect with others, to worship, and as an anthem for resistance in politics. In fact, the Smithsonian (n.d.) has noted that early in African American history, "music was a solace, a community-builder, and voice for hope during enslavement and afterward, in the days of Reconstruction and then Jim Crow" (para. 2). During slavery, the freedoms of Black people living in the Americas were restricted in many ways, so music passed down orally became a positive way for Black Americans to express themselves. Post-slavery, whether it be through jazz, rock 'n roll, the blues, the sounds of Motown, hip-hop, or R&B, music has been a way for Black people to continue to tell their stories, to lift their spirits, and to unite in protest (Smithsonian, n.d., para 1).

Music can inspire, empower, and encourage us to keep moving forward. When experiencing stress, music—like religious songs, for example—can remind us of what to do when we are in trouble, help us express our faith and gratitude, connect us to our ancestors, allow us to commune with God, and even give us hope for life after death (Hamilton et al., 2017). As it relates more specifically to empowerment, music can also help us to discuss collective responsibility and social injustice. A study conducted by Brooks and colleagues (2020), for example, explored messages about police brutality in rap music and found that this music validated the listeners' feelings, expressed a common desire that police who do harm to the Black community be punished, and highlighted the intergenerational legacy of victimization and wrongful manipulation by police. Similarly, research conducted by Tyson and his colleagues (2013) explored therapeutic messages in hip hop music and found themes that included social oppression, economic oppression, racial oppression, personal suffering, personal empowerment, praise of family values, praise of work and achievement, the importance of education, praise of women, spirituality, love, loyalty, and empathy. These findings reinforce the positive role music can have in providing an emotional release and emphasize the value of music as a tool for increasing critical consciousness and calling us to action.

While music can motivate and empower us, it is also true that at times, music can reinforce demoralizing and oppressive messages. The research conducted by Tyson and colleagues (2013) also found themes related to materialism and substance abuse, which in many ways has been harmful to the Black community. Moreover, research has also found that among Black women with weaker ethnic identity, exposure to rap music videos that depict thin-ideal images results in increased body dissatisfaction, increased drive for thinness, and even increased bulimia tendencies (Zhang et al., 2009). Therefore, when thinking about music as a tool for empowerment, it is important that you focus on music that uplifts and motivates you as opposed to music that makes you feel sad or think negatively about yourself. Accordingly, in this exercise, you will be asked to identify the music that empowers you. We hope that as you complete this exercise, the music you identify will provide nourishment for your soul and fortify you as you work to create positive change in your life.

1. What songs are currently on your playlist? What have you been listening to?

    _____

    _____

    _____

2. In what ways do these songs motivate or empower you?

    _____

    _____

    _____

3. If your songs are not empowering, what new songs can you add to your playlist? Try and think of songs that inspire or that encourage you to achieve your personal goals.

    _____

    _____

    _____

4. Lastly, how will you start using these songs as ways to positively cope? For example, if you're trying to change negative self-talk, think about beginning your morning with a song that has affirming words.

    _____

    _____

    _____

Your Task

Remember, what we hear impacts how we feel. Hearing negative messages, even in your music, can have a negative impact on your mood. Over the next week, be intentional about guarding what you hear. Find positive music that empowers you to be great.

Stories That Inspire

We as a Black community have a long tradition of storytelling. According to Kudakwashe Tuwe (2016), *storytelling* can be defined as "a method of recording and expressing feelings, attitudes, and responses to one's lived experiences" (p. 2). Different than simply reading a book out loud or reciting a story from memory, storytelling involves using the entire body—one's voice, body language, and facial gestures—to paint a picture that helps make sense of the world and forms a vision for future generations (Ngugi wa Thiong'o, 1986). In Africa, storytelling traditionally took place as part of family and community gatherings for entertainment, to communicate moral lessons, to pass along communal knowledge, to provide counsel, to impart wisdom, and to praise God (Tuwe, 2016). As such, the stories that were shared during these gatherings could in some ways be viewed as the roots that kept one's village culture alive. Accordingly, individuals gifted in storytelling were often revered as advisors and diplomats for the entire community (Britannica, n.d. a). In fact, in West African culture, the storytelling tradition was so important that a formal role was assigned to an individual in the community known as the *griot*, who was charged with preserving the genealogies, historical narratives, and oral traditions of the people (Britannica, n.d. b). To hear examples of the stories told by griots, you can listen to the African Folktale Podcast on Spotify or search out popular music featuring the works of artists considered to be modern-day griots, such as Omawumi and Lala Njava.

Throughout the African diaspora, the tradition of storytelling continued after the onset of the African slave trade as a way to preserve our past and culture, but also as a subversive tactic. In the Americas, enslaved Africans were not allowed to read or write. Storytelling in those times became a method our ancestors used to empower themselves to bear witness to what they had seen and heard, to cleverly tell stories of overcoming their enslavers, and to escape or rebel. Consider African American folktales featuring the character Brer Rabbit, for example. In the stories in which Brer Rabbit appears, the smaller, less powerful creature always outwits the larger, stronger characters such as Brer Bear and Brer Fox (Britannica, n.d. a, para 8). Metaphorically, Brer Rabbit represented the less powerful slaves and their desire to free themselves from their more powerful enslavers, represented by Brer Bear and Brer Fox. Today, the stories of Brer Rabbit, Brer Bear, and Brer Fox continue to live on, revived in new stories such as the *Tristan Strong* series by Kwame Alexander, as do other African American folktales such as those retold in *The Annotated African American Folktales* by Henry Louis Gates, Jr. and Maria Tatar. Through the ongoing telling of these stories, African Americans continue the tradition of using spoken word to convey empowerment messages relaying themes from all aspects of the human experience, particularly those related to making sense of the world, defiance and desire, and resistance (Gates & Tatar, 2017). Moreover, in the same spirit as our African relatives, these same themes are also brought to life through the stories of our modern-day storytellers in all genres of art, music, and literature.

To summarize, storytelling can be empowering, as it can help convey history, tell of triumph, and provide hope. In the exercise that follows, you will work to identify the stories that have and will empower you. As you read the following questions, think about stories you heard in your own childhood. These stories can be histories of your family members, African or African American folktales, stories you heard at school, or even cartoons. Feel free to choose whatever stories you like. The only requirement is that these stories are important to you and leave you with a sense of pride, motivation, or inspiration.

1. As a child, what were some of the stories that were read to you or that you read on your own that promoted a sense of pride? Feel free to even include stories that were made up by your family members and passed down to you. Write their titles here.

_____

_____

_____

2. What was it about these stories that inspired or motivated you?

_____

_____

_____

3. The children's tale *The Little Engine That Could* was an inspiring story with a message of never giving up. That message of never giving up can continue to empower us, even in our adulthood, when we face difficult times. Create some messages in the following space using the stories that inspire you.

_____

_____

_____

4. If you are spiritual or endorse a religious faith, what are some stories or characters from religious texts that empower you?

_____

_____

_____

5. How can you use these religious stories or characters to help you remain strong?

_____

_____

_____

Bonus: Now that you've identified ways that storytelling can foster empowerment in your own life, keep the tradition alive! Identify a young person to share your stories with, focusing on ways you can use these stories to teach, encourage, or inspire the young person to work toward achieving their own goals for their life.

Heritage Wall

In 2020, music icon Beyoncé released her second visual album titled, Black is King. Heralded by critics as a visual and lyrical masterpiece, this work of art featuring Afrobeats, African aesthetics, African themes, and African people was embraced by many in the Black community not only as an expression of Black pride, but also as an explicit rejection of conventional Eurocentric standards of beauty and culture. In one of the songs on the album, Black Parade, Beyoncé quips, "Ancestors on the wall, let the ghosts chit-chat" and goes on to explore the power and significance of embracing one's ancestral past through appreciation of the beauty, the art, the land, the people, and the sacrifices made by the people, including the members of your own family. Throughout this workbook we've also discussed the value of appreciating your cultural heritage, especially in terms of developing a strong sense of self and a core identity. *Heritage* can be defined as the history and achievements of one's cultural group (Küver, 2017). In this activity, we explore how appreciation of your cultural heritage through recognition of your family history can also be empowering. Our values, our beliefs, and the essence of who we are is often transmitted through our family members. Furthermore, as humans, we are designed to connect with other humans. Knowing your family history can provide a sense of connection to your ancestors, as well as the living members of your family. With this connection, we are able to draw on the strength, compassion, love, and other positive attributes we see in our family members as we forge our way forward in the face of adversities and life challenges.

Embracing Your Family Heritage

Without an understanding of your historical context, it's difficult to build a framework upon which to base your life. Your family stories can help you build this framework by allowing you to create your own narratives as you challenge negative messages about your communities and culture and discover various forms of empowerment. Connecting with the stories, life lessons, and proud moments of those who have come before us can also be encouraging. We both keep photographs of our grandparents in our offices and view them as a source of support as well as a reminder of the lessons and sacrifices of those who have gone before us. In this activity, you will be asked to develop your own heritage wall or table of people who came before you, so that you too can draw on your family history to help you feel confident and strong. Before starting this activity, let's begin with some questions that will help you build your wall or table area.

1. Who are the people in your family history with whom you feel close?

   _____

   _____

   _____

2. What is it about these individuals that you most identify with? What characteristics do you most connect with?

   _____

   _____

   _____

3. How might you use the memories of these individuals' strengths to empower yourself?

   _____

   _____

   _____

* We recognize that some of us have difficult or even traumatic family histories that make remembering family members painful. If this is the case for you, it may be beneficial to focus on a chosen family. A chosen family is a group of people you have intentionally chosen to embrace. These individuals may consist of friends, members of your place of worship, mentors, or others who have played a significant role in your life. As another alternative, you may also choose to complete your heritage wall using photos and other items representing members of the Black community whom you generally admire or find inspiring.

Creating Your Heritage Wall

Step one: Find an area of your home that you can call your "heritage wall or table."

Step two: Begin gathering pictures, artifacts, or memorabilia of the people you want to include on your wall or table. For this step, you might reach out to other family members that might have access to these items.

Step three: Create your heritage wall. Feel free to put your own unique touch on your heritage wall or table (e.g., this might be a quote or empowering statement). This is your personal area. Feel free to design it how you would like.

Step four: Think of how you might want to use your wall. For example, perhaps you might want to use your heritage wall and the surrounding area to meditate and ground yourself when you feel disempowered.

Final Reflection

After creating and using your heritage wall for a few days, reflect on the benefits this wall has provided in terms of serving as a source of support and empowerment. For example:

- ❏ What values are evident as you think about the history and achievements represented in the pictures and memorabilia included on your heritage wall?
- ❏ How can you use the values to guide you in your goals and efforts toward empowerment?
- ❏ How can you continue the legacy represented in your heritage wall?

My Pearls of Wisdom

Messages that are passed down to us from older generations can be empowering. As African Americans, we do not just inherit the wounds of racism—we also inherit wisdom. This wisdom can serve as medicine for healing and empowerment. Noted racialized trauma expert, Resmaa Menakem, for example, uses the wisdom he received from his grandmother as a basis for his bestselling book, *My Grandmother's Hands: Racialized Trauma and the Pathway to Mending Our Hearts and Bodies.* In this book, Menakem (2017) discusses strategies to heal from the pain of racialized trauma and describes the wisdom evidenced in his grandmother's habit of humming and rocking herself forward and backward and from side to side. According to Menakem (2017), while this habit seemed like little more than a ritual to comfort oneself, the behavior of humming and rocking actually involves a part of the body known as the *vagus nerve*, which is where we experience our emotions and a sense of relaxation or safety. By engaging in activities such as humming, rocking, or deep breathing, you can train yourself to consciously and deliberately relax, settle, and soothe your body during high-stress situations (Menakem, 2017).

Growing up, there may have been messages that were given to you as a child or behaviors you observed in your parents or grandparents that can be inspiring for you now. Some of these messages may even be attributed African proverbs, such as the saying, "It takes a village to raise a child." The following list gives some other examples of these messages and proverbs:

- ❏ "Don't take no wooden nickels"...meaning stand up for anything that's not right.
- ❏ "Don't look down on a man unless you're going to pick him up"...meaning never look down on someone unless you're going to help.
- ❏ "A hard head makes a soft behind"...meaning it's best to listen to the wisdom of your elders before you suffer the consequences of failing to take good advice.
- ❏ "Black people must stop acting like crabs in a barrel and work together"...meaning individuals should avoid hurting other members of their community in order to get ahead.
- ❏ "God don't bless mess"...meaning we shouldn't expect God to bless choices that go against His will.
- ❏ "Beauty is only skin deep"...meaning one's outward appearance is not nearly as important as the quality of their character.

Your Pearls of Wisdom

The examples just given were only a few of the pearls of wisdom that are commonly expressed in the Black community. In the oyster shell, write down pearls of wisdom you've received in your own life that can serve as empowering messages in your times of need. If you find yourself struggling to identify these messages, try asking friends or even using Google. The goal here is to collect these "pearls" to have handy when life gets overwhelming or you need strength to go on.

My Pearls of Wisdom

Release and Let Go

In spite of the wisdom and encouragement we receive from our elders and others around us, there are times we find ourselves thinking negative, disempowering thoughts. While it may be tempting to minimize these thoughts, we should be careful not to. There is power in our thinking. Whatever we think about and meditate on becomes our focus. Whatever we focus on, we usually end up doing. Therefore, the way we think can be one of the most significant sources of empowerment or disempowerment that we have. In order to anchor ourselves in thoughts that are more helpful and empowering, we must release thoughts that are negative and overly critical. In this activity, you will be asked to think of disempowering thoughts you need to release (i.e., let go of) and to develop replacement thoughts that will allow you to feel more capable and empowered in your life. Subsequently, you will also be asked to explore any behaviors you might have that are also disempowering. Begin by completing Table 31.1.

TABLE 31.1

Empowering Thoughts

Thoughts I Release	Thoughts I Accept
Example: "Things will never work out for me."	**Example:** "I accept the beautiful future God has planned for me and I let go of negativity."

Empowering Behavior

As you reflect on thoughts you need to release, it is also important to look at behaviors that are not empowering. These behaviors might be bad habits that stop you from living an abundant life and being your best self. Respond to the following questions to identify behaviors that are disempowering and then identify empowering behaviors you can replace them with.

1. Take a moment to reflect on any disempowering behaviors you might have. Here's a hint: These behaviors typically occur in response to disempowering thoughts. Write them down here.

   _____

   _____

   _____

   _____

   _____

   _____

2. Now reflect on empowering behaviors. What behaviors would you engage based on your empowering replacement thoughts?

   _____

   _____

   _____

   _____

   _____

   _____

Safe Spaces

In the current sociopolitical climate, it may seem that your humanity is not valued. Systemic racism goes unchecked in most segments of society and reports of racially motivated hate crimes continue to flood the news. Exposure to these events and the sense of devaluing that often follows can leave you feeling upset, or worse, with a sense of racialized trauma. How individuals cope with this trauma varies. Some may seek to avoid their feelings and become emotionally numb. Others live in the constant fear that something bad is going to happen to them or their loved ones. Regardless of one's specific coping response, being consumed with the unpleasant emotions such as fear, frustration, disappointment, and even anger can leave you in a position of feeling disempowered and overwhelmed. Developing safe spaces is one tool that has been found to help with managing these feelings because safe spaces provide a sense of empowerment and control. Therefore, this activity focuses on helping you to identify people, places, and events that leave you feeling physically, emotionally, and psychologically protected. However, before you begin, please read the following paragraph to learn more about safe spaces and the benefits they provide.

Most of us have relied on safe spaces throughout our lives. Think back to early childhood. Back then, some of your safe spaces may have been under your favorite blankie or in the arms of a parent or favorite relative. The specific type of safe space we are referring to in this activity is called a counterspace.

Copyright material from Janeé M. Steele and Charmeka S. Newton (2023) *Black Lives Are Beautiful*, Routledge

191

Counterspaces are defined as "sites where deficit notions of people of color can be challenged and where a positive climate can be established and maintained" (Solórzano et al., 2000, p. 70). Essentially, counterspaces are the places in which marginalized people experience an enhanced sense of wellbeing because they are (a) able to express their frustrations with negative cultural messages about their social group and (b) supported by the people who share the same group membership. According to research, there are many benefits associated with counterspaces. We've already identified enhanced psychological wellbeing and social support as two of these benefits. Other benefits include increased critical consciousness, greater cultural pride, a more positive sense of self, and more adaptive coping (Case & Hunter, 2012). For example, a study of African American women student affairs workers found that participation in professional counterspaces had a positive impact on their physical, spiritual, and interpersonal wellness, and increased opportunities for mentoring and networking (West, 2019). Similarly, a different study of African American male high schoolers found that the counterspace of an all-male educational setting helped participants of the study experience greater academic success, personal validation, and opportunities to think critically about race and their racialized experiences (Terry et al., 2014).

In your own life, counterspaces can play an important part in providing you with similar benefits. In the space that follows, we'd like for you to identify people, places, and events you can use as counterspaces. These people, places, and events may be formal or informal in nature. All that's important is that these places help you to feel safe and supported.

People (e.g., my spiritual leader or a group of friends)

_____

_____

_____

Places (e.g., my Zumba class or the barber shop)

_____

_____

_____

Events (e.g., a community concert that celebrates my race and culture)

_____

_____

_____

Bonus: Now that you have identified positive counterspaces in your life, think about how you can contribute to the safety and other benefits these places provide. If you are especially good at encouraging and validating others' feelings, be an encourager! Or, if you know of self-help books or mental health resources that facilitate healing from racialized trauma, be sure to share them with your peers. Let's all contribute to the growth and empowerment of our community by being a resource to each other.

Black Minds Matter

It is well document that professional help seeking within the Black community is low due to cultural stigma associated with counseling. For example, many Black families have the belief that "what happens in this house, stays in this house." Accordingly, individuals who were raised with this belief are often reluctant to share the intimate and personal details of their lives with a stranger, even if that stranger is a trained mental health professional.

Beyond cultural norms around privacy, other factors also contribute to mental health stigma and limited professional help seeking in the Black community. Some of these factors include low mental health literacy, masculinity norms, the strong Black woman schema, negative stereotypes about the type of individuals who receive therapy, and a belief that professional and religious coping strategies are incompatible (Jacoby et al., 2020; Watson & Hunter, 2015). A study conducted by Watson and Hunter (2015), for example, found that greater endorsement of the strong Black woman schema resulted in less psychological openness and less willingness to utilize mental health services. Likewise, in their study, Nelson and colleagues (2020) identified three negative outcomes associated with the strong Black woman schema and professional help seeking, which included masking or ignoring pain, an inability to ask for help, and lack of self-care. Among Black men, research has identified similar themes, as prior studies have found that internalized prejudice arising from stereotypes about mental health services is a deterrent from seeking psychological help for this group of men (Cadaret & Speight, 2018), as is fear of judgment from mental health professionals (Jacoby et al., 2020).

While overcoming the stigma associated with receiving mental health services can be difficult, there are many benefits to be gained if you do. Through culturally sensitive therapy, you can gain insight into the issues that contribute to your psychological distress, learn new coping strategies, and see a positive improvement to your mental health. This, in turn, can lead to an increased sense of control and empowerment in your life. Accordingly, this activity focuses on challenging and reframing some of the myths associated with mental health counseling.

❑ **Myth One**: Only crazy people seek mental health treatment.
The Truth: Seeking mental health treatment does not mean you're crazy. Many people seek mental health issues to address life transitions and adjustments. Most people dealing with mental health conditions just need some additional support. When people do struggle with more serious mental health concerns, therapy can actually be lifesaving.

❑ **Myth Two**: My information will be shared with others.
The Truth: Therapists are bound by certain laws, ethics, and rules of confidentiality that prohibit them from sharing your information with anyone that you do not authorize them to share your information with.

❑ **Myth Three**: Going to counseling means I don't trust Jesus.
The Truth: It is ok to have Jesus and a therapist too! Jesus empowers and equips people to help us. A therapist is one of those people, similar to a medical doctor. Seeking out a counselor does not mean you're not trusting Jesus.

Now, it's your turn. In the space provided here, list some of the concerns you have about entering into therapy.

_____

_____

_____

Given that there is so much stigma and so many myths around mental health treatment, how can you test out some of your concerns about entering into therapy?

_____

_____

_____

Bonus: Listed next are some suggestions to help you get started with therapy.

- ❏ Set up a phone or in-person consultation with a therapist to have your concerns answered.
- ❏ Go on psychologytoday.com and research therapists.
- ❏ Google Black therapy alliances or Black mental health alliances in your area.
- ❏ Contact your health insurance provider to find out more about your insurance benefits and mental health specialists who partner with your insurance.

Sociopolitical Empowerment

We all have a voice. Whether you use yours or not is up to you. In the past, African American activism in political, economic, and social spheres has resulted in significant advancements in laws and policies affecting our community. Examples of these laws and policies include the Civil Rights Act of 1964, the Voting Rights Act of 1965, and affirmative action. Today, sociopolitical activism continues to have a significant impact on the Black community. Some recent advancements in laws and policies affecting our quality of life and rights to self-determination include the CROWN Act, which protects against discrimination when wearing natural hair and the Matthew Sheppard and James Byrd Jr. Hate Crimes Prevention Act, which extends the reach of previous hate crime laws. Through these laws, and others like them, African Americans and other people of color are able to receive greater legal protections when confronted with systemic barriers to personal choice and power over one's life, which ultimately results in a greater sense of empowerment.

Like psychological and economic empowerment, sociopolitical empowerment can result in several benefits including greater community engagement and an increased sense of personal control (Livingston et al., 2017). Sociopolitical power involves using one's political voice to influence the state of governmental affairs. As seen with the 2008 Presidential election, change can occur, and hope can be reinstalled when people unite and exercise one source of sociopolitical power—the vote. However, voting is just one way in which we can use our sociopolitical voice. Use Table 34.1 to identify other ways in which you may or may not be activating your political voice. If you do the behavior listed, put a check mark in the "Yes" box. If you do not do the behavior listed, put a check mark in the "No" box.

TABLE 34.1
Finding Your Political Voice

Behavior	Yes	No
1. I voted in my most recent local election.		
2. I voted in the 2020 national election.		
3. I voted in the 2016 election.		
4. In the last one to two years, I've campaigned in a local or national election.		
5. I've persuaded others to vote through means like social media posts, yard signs, registering people to vote, or having conversations with people about voting.		
6. I've donated money to a political party.		
7. I'm a member of a political club or group (e.g., Young Democrats).		
8. I'm a part of a group that supports social change (e.g., Black Lives Matter, NAACP).		
9. I contact my local elected officials about issues within my community.		
10. I contact nonlocal or national elected officials about issues within my community.		
11. I understand the roles of the different branches of government.		

Reflection Questions
1. As you look at your sociopolitical chart, what areas are excelling as it relates to expressing your political voice? _____ _____ _____ 2. As you continue to look at your chart, what are areas for growth and improvement? _____ _____ _____

Your Task

Review Table 34.1 and your answers to the reflection questions and then come up with at least one goal to which you can commit to improve your socio-political voice. This goal should be accomplishable within the next two months.

Sample goal: I will go online and find out how to register to vote by or before this date: _____.

Sample goal: I will join a social club that will help me to exercise my political voice by or before this date: _____.

Your goal:

_____

_____

_____

Your Role as a Change Agent

In the prior activity, we discussed the importance of working toward sociopolitical empowerment. Through this activity, you were able to gain a greater understanding of your current level of sociopolitical empowerment and ways you can begin to increase this type of empowerment. The current activity continues the discussion of sociopolitical empowerment, focusing on one specific means of increasing your sense of sociopolitical empowerment—becoming a social change agent.

A *social change agent* is a person who takes action to make improvements in the lives of individuals and communities (Cobb, 2014). Taking action in your community by participating in politics, being involved in local organizations such as the NAACP, beautifying common spaces, protesting, or lobbying for needed resources are all examples of ways in which you can be a social change agent. As implied in the examples in Table 35.1, there are many different approaches one can take to be a social change agent. The following survey is based on George Lakey's (2016) typology of the different roles people can adopt to create social change. Gaining insight into the type of change agent role best suited to you can help you more clearly envision what work as a social change agent might look like for you specifically, increasing the likelihood of you engaging this type of behavior. Take a moment and answer the questions in the table to identify roles you might feel comfort in. Begin by answering "Yes" or "No" and do not worry about the score column until later.

TABLE 35.1

What Type of Change Agent Are You?

Questions	Yes	No	Score
1. I enjoy communicating with "the powerholders," people who can change a policy or practice.			
2. I am very likely to talk to an authority to correct an issue I felt was an injustice or problem.			
3. I enjoy building social connections to seek justice and evaluating how these efforts come to fruition to bring about social change.			
4. I enjoy providing direct service to individuals who are impacted by societal problems and personally doing what I can to help the situation.			
5. As a child I can remember playing the helper role to others, for example, standing up for someone who was being bullied.			
6. I enjoy helping those without privilege.			
7. I enjoy getting people who may not even know each other together and turning them into a well-oiled team.			
8. I enjoy pulling together resources to help others.			
9. I believe in the sheer power of numbers to create change.			
10. I do not mind creating a commotion to force powerholders to make a change.			
11. I would willingly be a part of a street protest or march to bring about social change.			
12. I'm willing to say things others may be afraid to say.			

Scoring Instructions: In the scoring column, give yourself a score of 1 for each question you answered "Yes" and a "0" for each question answered with a "No." Next, add your scores by placing your totals on the in the following list.

Questions 1 to 3: _____ (The Advocate)
Questions 4 to 6: _____ (The Helper)
Questions 7 to 9: _____ (The Organizer)
Questions 10 to 12: _____ (The Rebel)

Scoring Key: Any group of questions in which you have a score of 2 or higher indicates a social change role you might enjoy doing. Listed next are descriptions that correspond with each role.

❏ **The Advocate.** Advocates believe in engaging the legal system to create social change. For example, they may lobby or build coalitions to challenge unjust policies or procedures at a local or national level. They seek to give voice to the voiceless and the disempowered.

❏ **The Helper.** Helpers are motivated by the desire to provide direct service and to remedy societal problems. For example, they may help in developing programs for those who are unemployed by teaching them how to write resumes, or they may volunteer at the front desk of an organization that serves underrepresented groups. Helpers enjoy serving others.

❏ **The Organizer.** Organizers experience joy from gathering people around a common cause or theme. They tend to focus on coalition building to create change. Organizers often believe that there is power in numbers and that through strategically uniting massive amounts of people, they can influence the decisions of powerholders.

❏ **The Rebel.** Rebels believe in using protest and street activism as means to change. These individuals do not have issues with making a commotion to bring attention to unjust institutions or practices. The rebel will often use the strategic method of nonviolence to challenge people in power.

Reflection Questions

As you examine the four roles, it is not uncommon for you to notice that your preferences are represented by more than one role. Being aware of when and how you play each role is key to feeling a sense of empowerment. Knowing your purpose and operating within a role that is connected to your mission leads to intentionality and that in itself can be empowering. Conversely, operating outside of roles in which you feel comfortable may actually lead to a feeling of disempowerment. For example, if you are more of a helper, taking on the rebel role may create more anxiety and frustration than empowerment. Therefore, if you want to be an effective change agent, know your role and be sure to operate in ways that build your confidence and help you to feel stronger in your abilities and strengths.

1. In which change agent roles did you have the highest scores?

_____

_____

_____

_____

_____

_____

_____

2. To what extent do these results seem accurate for you?

_____

_____

_____

_____

_____

_____

_____

3. What are three specific ways you can engage these roles in your community?

_____

_____

_____

_____

_____

_____

_____

4. How would you personally benefit from engaging these roles in your community?

_____

_____

_____

_____

_____

_____

_____

5. How would your community benefit?

_____

_____

_____

_____

_____

_____

_____

_____

Black Economic Empowerment

Rev. Dr. Martin Luther King Jr. is well known for his "I Have a Dream" speech and his fight for racial equality. Yet did you know that Dr. King was also committed to achieving economic equality among the nation's poor? That's right. In 1967, Dr. King and members of the Southern Christian Leadership Conference (SCLC) put into motion a political agenda known as the Poor People's Campaign to highlight the problem of poverty in the United States and to find solutions to eradicate this social ill (Britannica, n.d. c). Using the battle-tested strategies of non-violent protest and civil disobedience, the primary feature of the Poor People's Campaign was a march on Washington, DC scheduled to take place daily from May 14 to June 28, 1968. The overarching goal of this march was to persuade Congress and the President to pass a $12 billion Economic Bill of Rights guaranteeing employment to those able to work, income to those unable to work, and an end to housing discrimination (Britannica, n.d. c). Inclusive of members from all racial backgrounds, it was hoped that this protest would be the largest and most successful social movement in U.S. history.

In the end, while the Poor People's Campaign did draw attention to the plight of poverty in the United States, it fell short of achieving its antipoverty legislation goals. Dr. King was assassinated two months before the march on Washington, DC took place, national guardsmen were mobilized to stop protestors just five days after the march began, and few gains were made in reducing economic disparities in the United States (Britannica, n.d. c). Accordingly, many scholars describe economic equality as "the unfinished business of the civil rights struggle" (Nembhard, 2008, p. 758). In the Black community, the "unfinished business" of economic equality is an especially significant aspect of empowerment because it's a means through which we can gain purchasing power and a seat at decision making tables. Unfortunately, participation in mainstream economic models (e.g., self-help reliant primarily upon charity or assimilating into existing economic structures) has resulted in little success for the majority of African Americans (Nembhard, 2008). Therefore, scholars argue that alternative approaches are needed to bolster

TABLE 36.1
Support Black-Owned Businesses

Community cooperation is essential to achieving economic empowerment within the Black community. By committing to patronizing businesses owned by Black entrepreneurs, you play a vital role in strengthening the Black economy and achieving Black economic agency.	
Service/business	**Places I could support**
Beauty supply stores	
Restaurants	
Mortgage or realtor company	
Groceries	
Auto-repair	
Clothing	
Home repair	
Family fun zones (e.g., bowling alleys, game centers)	
Craft supplies	
Jewelry	
Audio/videography/technology	

Black economic power and agency. Chief among these approaches is entrepreneurship and supporting Black businesses. By supporting Black businesses, members of the Black community have the opportunity to help "lift the burden of economic exploitation" (Reddix, 1974, p. 119). Moreover, supporting Black-owned businesses can create a sense of pride in supporting people from your own racial background.

In this activity, you will identify Black businesses in your community you would feel comfortable supporting on some level. In Table 36.1, write the names of the African American business you could start or will continue to support. As you think about this, be sure to consider companies that are small start-ups or storefront facilities.

Bonus: If you do not know where you can shop Black-owned businesses, there are many useful directories to assist you. Examples of these directories include Shoppe Black (shoppeblack.us) and Official Black Wall Street (obws.com). Try using these directories to locate local, national, and global Black-owned brands. Additionally, if you are a business owner, try listing your company on these websites to increase the options available to consumers.

Messages About Money

Money is one of the most important resources determining quality of life. With money, we're able to do things like enjoy travel, provide for our families, and help those in need. Yet, in spite of the many benefits money provides, most of the messages about money we receive in life aren't positive. Consider the following sayings:

- ❏ "Money is the root of all evil."
- ❏ "Mo' money, mo' problems."
- ❏ "Money doesn't grow on trees."

Negative messaging about money is common throughout American society. Unfortunately, in the Black community, messages of this kind only worsen pre-existing disparities in economic status. According to the U.S. Census Bureau (2018), White families typically have higher incomes than Black families, with the median family income of Black families being less than 60 percent of White households. In the previous activity, we discussed steps Black people can take as a community to address socioeconomic disparities through cooperative economics and shopping at Black-owned businesses. Another way you can begin to empower yourself as it relates to socioeconomic status is by challenging and reframing negative messages you have around money. Therefore, this activity is designed to help you increase awareness of your attitudes about money and their impact on your life. First, you will complete reflection questions exploring your experiences with money. Then, you will complete a checklist of key money habits and indicators of economic empowerment. At the end of this activity, you will identify goals to implement new money habits in your life based on this checklist and what you learned about your attitudes toward money.

1. What is your first memory of money?

    _____

    _____

    _____

2. What messages were given to you about money as you grew up?

    _____

    _____

    _____

3. What is the most difficult thing about money for you now?

    _____

    _____

    _____

4. To what extent did your family equip you to be money-wise?

    _____

    _____

There's no denying that because of slavery and systemic racism, Black people are at a socioeconomic disadvantage when compared to their White counterparts. There is little we can do to put right this history. The talk of reparations has long been discussed for the reconciliation of the 400 years of slavery that was imposed on African Americans, but no action has been taken to make a reparation plan a reality. Therefore, we as a people cannot wait for our government to level the playing field. We must work to level it ourselves. And while economic growth will not fully correct or heal the centuries of misdeeds inflicted on the Black community, it could be a step in the right direction in terms of empowering this group to have more equal opportunities to determine their quality of life.

TABLE 37.1

Money Habit Checklist

Questions	Yes	No
1. I have money set aside for an emergency fund or a "rainy day."		
2. I worry about being able to pay my bills and expenses.		
3. I save some of the income I earn each pay period.		
4. I track my income and spending.		
5. I am behind on some of my bills.		
6. I know what resources are available for me in my community if I needed financial help.		
7. My credit history has made it hard for me to obtain a car loan, mortgage, phone, or job.		
8. I spend too much on things that are not an investment, that is, leisure items versus items I can earn revenue from.		
9. I have a college fund set up for my children or future children.		
10. I have a retirement account (e.g., a 401k).		
11. I understand how my retirement account works.		
12. I have a plan for advancing in my career.		

Ideally, you were able to gain insight into some of the negative messages you received in life that may be influencing your attitudes toward money. The checklist in Table 37.1 provides a more objective indicator of where you are with money. Work on completing this checklist with an open and compassionate mind. The goal of the checklist is not to criticize your money habits. Instead, this checklist is designed to give you credit for what you are already doing well, and to provide some ideas about next steps you can take to grow in this area even more.

Final Reflection

As you look at the questions to which you answered "No," take a moment and reflect upon what steps you can take to turn some of your no's into yes's. For example, if you do not have a retirement account set up perhaps you could talk to your human resource department or a finical advisor to learn how to set one up. Take a few moments and in the space provided here, reflect upon how you build your economic empowerment by setting some specific tangible goals for yourself. Check back periodically and write down how you are doing with this goal.

Sample goal: I will set up a 401k by or before this date: _____.

Your goal:

_____

_____

_____

_____

_____

_____

Progress with your goal:

_____

_____

_____

_____

_____

_____

Anti-Racism Empowerment Strategies

Facing racism and the perceived inability to respond to racism can lead to feelings of disempowerment. According to Prilleltensky and Gonick (1996), another word for this specific type of disempowerment is surplus powerlessness. *Surplus powerlessness* can be defined as the belief that you are more limited in your ability to create change than you actually are. In thinking about this definition, it is important to distinguish between real and surplus powerlessness (Lord & Hutchison, 1993). Real powerlessness occurs when individuals experience inequalities and reduced self-determination due to specific laws and policies. We listed examples of these policies in the introduction to this part of the workbook. Some of them included unfair lending practices, biased policing and criminal sentencing, voter suppression, and inequitable funding of schools. Surplus powerlessness, on the other hand, is an internalized belief that change cannot occur, resulting in apathy and an unwillingness to advocate for more control (Lord & Hutchison, 1993). For people of color and other oppressed groups, surplus powerlessness can have the devasting effect of allowing racism to go unchecked, even when there is a chance to lessen it or hold those in positions of power accountable (Prilleltensky & Gonick, 1996). Moreover, surplus powerlessness can also lead to feelings of anxiety, guilt, and self-disappointment when individuals want to confront oppression but do not know how to (Sue et al., 2019). Failing to act when we hear racist jokes, when it's time to vote in local elections, or when we notice disparate access to resources are just a few of the ways many of us exhibit surplus powerlessness on an everyday basis.

While speaking out against racism and discrimination can be empowering, we recognize that doing so can be overwhelming, especially when you feel as though you do not have the tools or skills necessary to speak out. Therefore, we want to acknowledge that steps toward empowerment should be balanced with self-care. Examples of self-care strategies when dealing with racial oppression typically include social support, spirituality and religion, humor, positive self-talk, and withdrawing (Sue et al., 2021). However, scholars also suggest that directly or indirectly confronting racism can also be a form of self-care when dealing with racial oppression (Obear, 2017). Drawing on this suggestion, this activity focuses on providing you with anti-racism tools called microinterventions (Sue et al., 2019), which you can use to increase your sense of power and ability to respond when targeted with racism.

What is Anti-Racism?

As mental health professionals, we tend to focus on the psychological impact of racism. This is because racism has severe emotional consequences for people of color, including depression, anxiety, guilt, humiliation, and self-alienation (Carter, 2007). Yet, while the emotional consequences of racism can be difficult, and sometimes even traumatic, another and perhaps even more devasting consequence of racism is that when it is internalized, racism can make its targets respond in ways that actually perpetuate limitations to resources and power. For example, surplus powerlessness along with learned helplessness, avoidance, and conformity to White cultural standards and norms are all behaviors that contribute to racist views and policies going unchallenged and being seen as the norm (Prilleltensky & Gonick, 1996; Steele & Newton, 2022). In order to experience greater levels of empowerment, it is important that we recognize the ways in which our behaviors reinforce racism and begin to instead be antiracist.

In his book *How to be an Antiracist*, Ibram X. Kendi (2019) defines an *antiracist* as "one who is supporting an antiracist policy through their actions or expressing an antiracist idea" (p. 13). Essentially, anti-racism involves actively challenging racist policies and practices through your words or behaviors. This is different than being nonracist, which refers to personally refraining from racially prejudiced attitudes or behaviors. Consider an example from our local community to illustrate this point. During the height of the COVID-19 pandemic, vaccination centers were setup around town at schools and businesses to encourage members of the community to receive their vaccinations by making it easier for them to do so. A pastor of a church on a lower income and located in a predominantly Black side of town noticed that no vaccination centers had been established in this part of the community, despite the fact that these members of the community were statistically the most affected by COVID-19. Recognizing this, the pastor used his position in the community to bring this oversight to the attention of the county health department and city officials. As a result, vaccination centers were immediately established at multiple locations in this part of town, increasing access to the COVID-19 vaccine. In this example, a nonracist attitude on the pastor's part would have been to simply refrain from subscribing to the assumption that all Black people don't want the vaccine. Instead, the pastor's antiracist approach led him to take action that actually resulted in the elimination of a practice that was limiting access to an important resource in the local Black community, the COVID-19 vaccine.

Microinterventions

In the previous example, the instance of racism described occurred at the macro, city-wide level. For people of color and other cultural minority groups, smaller, everyday insults known as microaggressions can also contribute to psychological distress and a feeling of disempowerment. *Microaggressions* are subtle, often unintentional, put downs that reflect prejudiced or discriminatory messages (Sue & Sue, 2016). Originally, this term was coined by an African American psychiatrist named Chester Pierce in the 1970s. Since then, this term has been popularized within the mental health profession by Derald Wing Sue and his colleagues.

According to Sue and Sue (2016), there are three specific types of microaggressions: (1) microinsults, (2) microassaults, and (3) microinvalidations. *Microinsults* refer to unintentional comments or behaviors that demean a person's heritage or social identity, while *microassaults* are comments, behaviors, or environmental cues that more overtly convey discriminatory messages. The other type of microaggressions, *microinvalidations*, refers to comments or behaviors that negate or dismiss the cognitive, affective, or experiential realities of individuals from marginalized backgrounds. Telling a Black person that they "speak so well," using the word *ghetto* to describe African American vernacular (AAVE), and comments such as "When I look at you, I don't see color," are examples of microinsults, microassaults, and microinvalidations, respectively. While seemingly innocuous, these types of comments, behaviors, and environmental cues create hostile social climates that contribute to the persistently high levels of stress and fatigue among people of color (Sue et al., 2019).

To arm targets of microaggressions with strategies to combat these put downs, Sue and his colleagues (2019, 2021) developed the concept of microinterventions. *Microinterventions* are defined as:

the everyday words or deeds, whether intentional or unintentional, that communicate to targets of microaggressions (a) validation of their experiential reality, (b) value as a person, (c) affirmation of their racial or group identity, (d) support and encouragement, and (e) reassurance that they are not alone.

(Sue et al., 2019, p. 134)

They include three distinct types of action that include: (1) microaffirmations, (2) microprotections, and (3) microchallenges (Sue et al., 2021). *Microaffirmations* are small acts that affirm an individual's identity, life experiences, or worth. Examples of microaffirmations include statements designed to support targets of discrimination, such as the anti-racist statements put out by many organizations in the wake of recent social unrest and police brutality, or words of validation commonly shared among targets and allies such as "I see you" (Steele & Lee, 2022). *Microprotections* refer to proactive efforts to teach others about racism, to promote cultural pride, or to equip others to challenge bias and discrimination. These interventions occur between members of the same social identity and include traditional empowerment strategies such as consciousness-raising and teaching skills to deal with racism. Finally, *microchallenges* are direct actions taken to challenge biased and oppressive behaviors, policies, and practices. They may include directly confronting perpetrators, social advocacy, and civil disobedience such as protests or boycotts (Sue et al., 2021).

Microinterventions can provide those who are impacted by racially motivated comments with a sense of control and self-efficacy. In this exercise, we will define and provide an opportunity for you to practice three of Sue et al.'s (2019) specific microinterventions: (1) make the invisible visible, (2) disarm the microaggression, and (3) educate the perpetrator. Begin by reading the definition of each strategy, the example scenario, and the hidden message. Then, develop your own response in the column labeled "Your Response." A sample response is given in case you feel stuck.

TABLE 38.1
Fighting Back with Microinterventions

Speaking out against racism and discrimination can be empowering. Yet, sometimes knowing exactly how to respond to racism and discrimination can be challenging. Below, you will find three microinterventions designed to help you respond to a specific type of racial discrimination known as microaggressions. Read and complete the chart to practice developing this skill so that you can use it in the daily situations you experience.

Make the Invisible Visible
Acknowledging the stereotype that is embedded within the comment or action and challenging what has been said or done by bringing the offense to the forefront or forcing the person to consider the impact of what they have done.

Scenario	Hidden Message	Sample Response	Your Response
A Black man is seated next to a White heterosexual couple in a restaurant. When the White woman notices the Black man, she moves her wallet and phone away from the man.	Black men are criminals and cannot be trusted.	"It's okay, I'm not a thief." "Did you notice what you did when I sat down?"	

Disarm the Microaggression
Communicating your disagreement with what was said or done and immediately refuting the actions or words.

Scenario	Hidden Message	Sample Response	Your Response
A fellow African American colleague, Kara, is giving a presentation. After the presentation you overhear one of your White colleagues commenting on Kara's presentation, stating, "You know Kara speaks so well, sometimes I forget she's Black. You know, she's so different than other Blacks."	Black people are not as educated or articulate as White people.	"Ouch. You know that is a really hurtful comment. It really makes me feel uncomfortable hearing you say that."	

(continued)

TABLE 38.1 Cont.

Educate the Perpetrator			
Appealing to the value system of the perpetrator, pointing out commonalities, fostering awareness, and promoting empathy.			
Scenario	Hidden Message	Sample Response	Your Response
A Black man, Stephen, is at a planning meeting for his child's school. At the meeting, the parents discuss a basketball fundraiser to raise money for the school. One of the White parents says, "Stephen I really think you should chair the basketball fundraiser committee. I'm sure you know a lot about the sport, and I think this role will fit you."	Black people lack diversity of interests and skills.	"You know, despite stereotypes, not all Black people like or can play basketball. Within the Black community, there is diversity—there's not a one size fits all model. That's probably true for your community as well."	

Bonus: Sometimes negative thoughts or expectations prevent individuals from implementing changes in their lives. Confronting racism can be a daunting task and it is easy to be overwhelmed. Before attempting to implement microinterventions, first identify any negative thoughts you might have about using this skill. Then, develop positive reframes for these thoughts. Write them both in the space provided.

_____

_____

_____

_____

_____

_____

_____

_____

PART 5

Tools to Promote Community

DOI: 10.4324/9781003221357-44

How do you define community? While seemingly a simple question, the answer to this query is actually quite complex when it comes to the Black community, as there is no monolithic view of what this community entails. For some, the defining characteristics of the Black community vary and depend upon the timeframe one examines. For example, some people view the Black community as being more cohesive and united during the 1950s and 1960s, prior to desegregation. For individuals with this view, living in closer physical proximity to each other provided more opportunities for greater community control, a stronger Black economy, and more self-determined social institutions (Glasgow, 1972). This, in turn, allowed the Black community to be more strongly characterized by cooperation, a common purpose, and collective responsibility.

Since desegregation, how we define the Black community is arguably more diverse, as Black people now have more residential and economic stratification. Nevertheless, there are certain traditions, cultural rituals, holidays, languages, and institutions that continue to distinguish us from other races. So, while our experiences may be different across generations, there are things that help us create a sense of community and shape the experience of being Black in the United States and across the globe.

Regardless of how you define it, having a sense of community is important in the protection of your emotional and psychological wellbeing. Research shows that being part of a community increases an individual's sense of belonging and lets us know that we matter to others (Yap et al., 2011). Conversely, when belongingness and mattering are lacking, emotional and psychological reactions to prejudice and discrimination may be intensified, and individuals may experience an adverse impact on their functioning in academic, occupational, or social settings. To illustrate these ideas, we'd like to share some of our own experiences with community.

Dr. Char's First Community Experiences

Growing up in the metro Detroit area, Char's first experiences of community really began on Griggs Street, where her maternal grandparents lived. Griggs Street is located in Detroit, right off of Eight Mile Road. Eight Mile is a significant marker because it indicates the starting point of the inner-city community of Detroit. Growing up in a two-parent working class family, Char and her siblings were often taken care of by her grandparents while her parents worked. Thus, it was at her grandparents' house on Griggs Street that she saw community life play out for the first time. Char's grandparents had strong relationships with the neighbors that lived on their block and she would often see her grandparents take care of and meet the needs of their fellow neighbors, whether it was by her grandfather mowing the yards of older neighbors in the community or by her grandmother cooking a southern meal for the neighbor across the street who had suffered a stroke and was immobile. At an early age, Char saw community defined as a place where people share resources, show love, and take care of one another.

Char's other significant memory of the Black community was through her experience with the Black church. Char attended one of the larger Black Baptist churches in Detroit, and it was there that Char first learned that a religious organization could foster a sense of support, community, and development of one's racial identity. While attending this church, Char met a youth director by the name of Mrs. Hattie Knox. Mrs. Knox took a special interest in nurturing youth in the community. She gave Char some of her first public speaking opportunities by allowing Char to speak at different youth conferences and youth day events. It was through Mrs. Knox that Char built confidence in herself and her ability to speak in public. It was also through the Black church that Char saw how religious institutions could help the people in her community have hope and a sense of power in a world that often denies them power.

Reflecting back on her early community experiences, Char realizes that these experiences have shaped Char into the person she is today. Her desire to help others in the Black community started on Griggs Street when she saw her grandparents helping others, while her desire to help install hope in others, to present, and to speak started in her church community. Thus, these early experiences in the Black community were crucial in her development as a person.

Dr. Janeé's First Community Experiences

Janeé's experiences with community are more mixed than Char's. During elementary school, Janeé lived in a residential community that was primarily Black but also lower in socioeconomic status when compared to the White peers she went to school with. Thus, early in life, Janeé in some ways equated being Black with being poor, which was difficult. At the end of middle school, however, Janeé moved to a community that was more racially and economically diverse. This allowed Janeé to see greater similarities across races, which ironically freed her to more fully embrace the unique aspects of her own race and culture.

Two conduits for community Janeé experienced during this time were her school peers and her church. In high school, everyone had their personal cliques and besties but the Black students in the school, for the most part, all banded together and supported each other—nerds, jocks, and average Joes alike. For Janeé, who is a shy person, this approach to Black community taken by the students at her school was important because it provided a sense of belonging and acceptance she might have otherwise struggled to find. It also allowed Janeé to participate in everyday aspects of Black culture—things like music, fashion, and dance—which may seem trivial in some regards but in other ways reflect the deeper meanings of the shared experiences of the larger Black community. Music was an especially salient aspect of Black community for Janeé at this time because it sparked larger conversations about violence and misogyny in our culture, especially after the deaths of Tupac and Biggie, which, in turn, led to even larger conversations about the Black community's tradition of care and protection for each other and the extent to which we were losing that. In a similar way, Janeé's connection to the Black church also prompted larger reflections on the state of the Black community, as the church's youth regularly participated in events focused on the Black experience and securing a better future for new generations.

> ### How Do You Define Community?
> Take a moment and reflect on some of your own early experiences within the Black community. As you do, consider the following questions:
>
> - ❑ What experiences have the greatest impact on your view of the Black community?
> - ❑ How have the experiences shaped your development as a Black person?
> - ❑ How can community be used as a tool to heal from racialized trauma?
>
> Keep these answers in mind as you complete this final part of the workbook.

Reflecting on her early experiences, Janeé realizes her view of community is heavily defined by a sense of collective responsibility and care for one another. For Janeé, this sense of responsibility and care is the very pulse of the Black community, and a significant motivator in all aspects of her life, at home, at work, and with others.

Community as a Tool for Healing

As mentioned, community offers a sense of belonging and mattering, which can increase one's sense of wellbeing and offer protection against negative emotional and psychological reactions to prejudice and discrimination (Yap et al., 2011). Reflection of the value of community can also create a sense of pride and pinpoint areas in which you may need to heal if there has been hurt that has occurred from community life.

In this part of the workbook, we will look at the role of community in positive racial identity development and healing from racial trauma, emphasizing strengths and resources that may be drawn upon from within your community. Accordingly, activities in this part focus on defining what it means to be Black, with the goal of (a) articulating the depth, richness, and variety of traditions among Black people throughout the diaspora, and (b) countering false, mono-lithic views of the Black community. Activities in this part also explore how to ask for help and seek support when needed, as well as the importance of being trustworthy and giving back to the community. Sacred people and places that traditionally offer safety and community are highlighted, and the part is concluded with activities to help you reflect on your place in the Black community and broader society in the light of the insights and self-discovery accomplished by completing this workbook.

Finding Your Tribe

As mentioned in the introduction to this part of the workbook, one of the biggest benefits of community is the sense of belonging it provides. *Belongingness* can be defined as the extent to which an individual feels personally accepted, respected, included, and supported by others in their social environment (Goodenow & Grady, 1993, p. 80). Another closely related term is mattering. *Mattering* can be defined as the experience of feeling significant to others (Tucker et al., 2010). When belongingness and mattering are lacking, emotional and psychological reactions to prejudice and discrimination may be intensified, and individuals may experience an adverse impact on their functioning in academic, occupational, or social settings (Adejumo, 2021; Boston & Warren, 2017). Conversely, increasing one's sense of belongingness and mattering can serve as a protective factor, as these constructs result in more positive racial identity (Yap et al., 2011), self-determination, self-definition, self-acceptance, and self-love (Johnson, 2016).

This activity is designed to increase the sense of belongingness and mattering you experience through community by helping you to find your tribe. A tribe can be described as individuals who have your back, offer social-emotional support, help you deal with race-based issues, and encourage you. As you go through the process of finding your tribe by completing the following steps, keep in mind that your tribe should be an intimate/small group of people, at most five people.

Finding Your Tribe

Step one: Identify the characteristics you would like your tribe members to have. Write them down in the space provided.

_____

_____

_____

Step two: Identify what you hope to take from the tribe (e.g., validation or mentorship to start your own business) and what you can give to members (e.g., encouragement and support or the benefits of one of your talents or skills).

_____

_____

_____

Step three: Identify tribe members for the different domains of your life, for example, work, church, neighborhood.

_____

_____

_____

Step four: If you're not able to identify people you can include in your tribe, brainstorm ways you can connect with others. Examples include volunteer, join a community group that supports your racial identity, or join a ministry at your place of worship where you can meet others.

_____

_____

_____

Step five: Find ways you can nurture the development of your tribe, for example, monthly in-home meet-ups to check-in with one another about your experiences connected to issues around race and racism.

_____

_____

_____

Final Reflection

South African leader Bishop Desmond Tutu often spoke of the philosophy "ubuntu." Ubuntu is a principle that translates to "a person is a person through other persons." In the space provided, reflect upon what this philosophy means to you, and more specifically, what the implications of this philosophy are for you as you work to establish your tribe.

_____

_____

_____

_____

_____

_____

_____

_____

_____

_____

_____

_____

_____

_____

_____

_____

_____

_____

_____

Cultural Institutions

Cultural institutions can be defined as public organizations that exist primarily for the purpose of preserving and promoting a group's culture and heritage (Gutiérrez & Creekmore, 2013). As such, cultural institutions are an important means through which a community's values, history, language, norms, and behaviors are passed on from one generation to the next (Johnson & Carter, 2020). In the Black community, examples of cultural institutions include the church, civic organizations such as the NAACP, local community centers, and formal spaces dedicated to the transmission of Black cultural knowledge such as museums, libraries, and historically Black colleges and universities.

Participation in Black cultural institutions can contribute to your psychological health and wellbeing by fostering a sense of community and teaching you important coping strategies like faith and prayer (Johnson & Carter, 2020). Cultural institutions can also help foster positive racial socialization and identity development by promoting racial pride and preparing individuals to deal with racial bias. Unfortunately, there are many reasons individuals might not always take advantage of the benefits cultural institutions have to provide. Some of us were not exposed to many of these institutions while growing up. Being creatures of habit, we sometimes do not move outside of our comfort zone or the things we are familiar with to explore what our community may have to offer. Others may have experienced hurt in some of these institutions. For example, *church hurt*, which is defined as pain inflicted by religious institutions, has caused many individuals to turn away from participation in the church as a cultural institution. In these cases, while the decision to remove oneself from the church is made in an attempt to protect oneself from this hurt, it often has adverse side effects such as feeling cut off from a significant source of community and coping.

The goal of this activity is to help you foster a stronger sense of community by identifying cultural institutions local to your area. In the following list, you will find several questions designed to help you do this. As you respond to each question, feel free to do additional research to fill in any information you might not currently have. Additionally, if you have experienced hurt in any cultural institutions, try talking to a family member, friend, therapist, or other trusted person to help you deal with this hurt. It can also be helpful to remember that not all organizations are the same. If you experience hurt with one specific group of people, it is very possible to find a different group with values and behaviors more consistent with what you desire.

1. What are some of the prominent cultural institutions within your community (e.g., church, non-profit organizations, NAACP)?

   _____

   _____

   _____

2. What needs do you have currently?

   _____

   _____

   _____

3. Which of the intuitions listed in response to question 1 might help you meet the needs you listed in question 2?

   _____

   _____

   _____

4. How can you engage these community institutions to see about getting your needs met?

_____

_____

_____

5. If your needs cannot be met in your local community, how can you creatively find ways to meet your needs? One example might be to join a social media group that has broader geographic reach in the Black community.

_____

_____

_____

Bonus: As mentioned, cultural institutions include places that document, interpret, and facilitate engagement with one's cultural heritage. Examples of these institutions include museums such as the Smithsonian National Museum of African American History and Culture in Washington, DC and libraries such as the Obama Presidential Center, located on the Southside of Chicago. As a bonus, plan a field trip to one of these locations or a museum or library local to you. As you visit the institution, reflect on how the information presented by the organization contributes to your sense of community and racial pride. You can try asking yourself questions such as:

❏ How does the information presented in this institution contribute to my sense of Black pride and community?
❏ How does the information presented in this institution broaden my understanding of how we got to where we are today?
❏ How can I use this understanding as inspiration or motivation when faced with struggles in my own life?

The Hate They Give

In 2017, author Angie Thomas's debut novel, *The Hate U Give*, was released to wide critical acclaim. Inspired by the Black Lives Matter movement, this book told the fictional story of Starr, a teenaged girl whose friend was murdered by the police. While the novel grapples with many sources of pain in the Black community, one of the issues explored was how racially biased and prejudiced messaging contributes to negative views of the Black community. In this activity, we invite you to identify and challenge these messages in order to reframe any negative internalized views you may have about the Black community. Begin by first drawing pictures or writing words that depict the hate or negative message the media and dominant culture give about the Black community. After this, you'll have an opportunity to refute these messages with positive counterexamples.

The Hate They Give

Reflection Question
1. As you look at what you have constructed, how does it make you feel?

Now it's your turn to counteract the hateful messages that are often given about the Black community by drawing a picture or using words to show all the things you love about the Black community. What makes you proud of your community? Draw it in the following space.

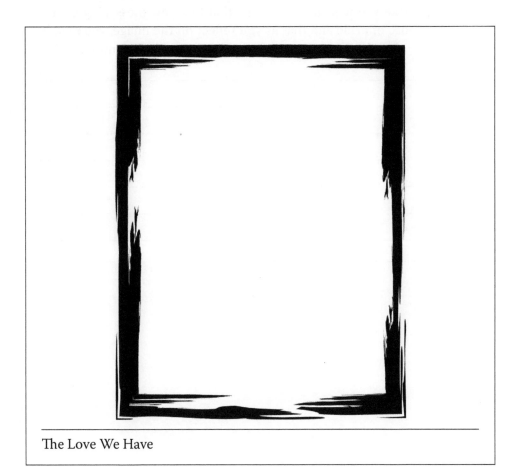

The Love We Have

Reflection Question

2. As you look at the new picture you have constructed, how does this image make you feel? It is our hope that this new messaging brings you a sense of pride and that as you reflect on the image, you're able to remember the greatness that lives within the Black community.

_____

_____

_____

_____

_____

_____

_____

Contribute Your Gift

The desire to give back to the community is common among many Black people (McCallum, 2017). According to social science researcher, Carmen McCallum (2017), this desire is in large part connected to *collectivism*, which is defined as a cultural orientation that values the needs of others over the needs of the individual. Collectivism can be best understood as part of a broader Afrocentric worldview that emphasizes cooperation, interdependence, the collective, responsibility of the individual to the group, harmony with other living things, and balance within one's own existence. In your own life, you may know individuals who live according to Afrocentric principles to varying degrees; yet research suggests that even Black people who are estranged from African traditions and customs nevertheless exhibit parallel customs and traditions such as close relationships with extended family, respect for old age, honoring the ancestors, and creating pathways for future generations (McCallum, 2017; Shipp, 1983). Accordingly, no matter how much one consciously recognizes the presence of Afrocentric values in their life, remnants of this value system nevertheless have an important impact on how we view and relate to the world.

Given the importance of collectivism in the Afrocentric worldview, one of the most potent ways to create a sense of community is to involve yourself with other people by giving back and doing something you value in an organized way. This activity is designed to help you think of ways you can create a sense of community by contributing your gifts to others. Through answering the following questions, it is hoped that you will be able to develop a plan to contribute more to your community.

1. Think of an activity you value (e.g., a hobby or a skill you have). Write it down in the following space.

   _____

   _____

   _____

2. Next, write down what makes you passionate about this hobby or skill.

   _____

   _____

   _____

3. Now, identify how might you share this hobby or skill with others. Listed here are some ideas that might provoke some thoughts on how you might share this skill within your community.

   ❑ Volunteer at a non-profit
   ❑ Organize a community-wide event with people who share your hobby or skill
   ❑ Create a blog or social media page dedicated to your hobby/skills and share it with people in your community
   ❑ Join a board of directors that promotes your interest area

   _____

   _____

   _____

4. Now, develop a goal describing how and when you will share your hobby and skill. Once you have done it, come back to this page and write about doing so and how it made you feel.

   _____

   _____

   _____

Juneteenth

The acknowledgment of holidays within our community is significant because it is through these acknowledgements that we can commemorate important moments in our history. One long-celebrated holiday in the Black community is Juneteenth. According to History.com, Juneteenth, short for "June Nineteenth," marks the day when federal troops arrived in Galveston, Texas in 1865 to take control of the state and ensure that all enslaved people were freed, a full 2½ years after the signing of the Emancipation Proclamation (Nix, 2021). While historians date the first Juneteenth celebration back to Texas in 1866, it did not become a federally recognized holiday until June 17, 2021. Accordingly, Juneteenth is considered the longest-running African American holiday, as well as the first new federal holiday since MLK Day was adopted in 1983.

Beyond recognition of freedom from slavery, Juneteenth is often utilized as a time to celebrate African American culture broadly. As such, Juneteenth celebrations typically focus on family and may take place in the form of barbeques, festivals, picnics, church services, or other similar gatherings. This activity will give you an opportunity to research how the activity is celebrated in your community this coming year so that you might plan how you would like to recognize this day.

1. How does your community celebrate Juneteenth? Google or social media platforms such as Facebook can be helpful in locating this information.

_____

_____

_____

2. What are some ways you personally would like to celebrate the day? Some ideas may be to organize a dinner with close friends/family and have a discussion around the day or our history, to watch a move, to support a Black-owned business, or to donate to a Black non-profit in your community.

_____

_____

_____

Seven Principles

As descendants of people stolen from their land and heritage, many of us have been separated from African customs and traditions. Kwanzaa is a holiday that was designed to reconnect people of African descent in the United States to values and principles that are reflective of broader African culture (Greenspan, 2021). Kwanzaa takes place each year from December 26 to January 1.

What is Kwanzaa, Exactly?

While many African Americans are familiar with Kwanzaa, some are not. This is in large part due to the fact that Kwanzaa is not a religious holiday, but a cultural one (Greenspan, 2021). In fact, Kwanzaa was first started by a Black nationalist named Dr. Maulana Karenga in 1966 as a way to unite and empower the African Americans in his community who were dealing with the aftermath of the Watts riots. Since that time, Kwanzaa has become widely embraced throughout the country, celebrated through both community events and family gatherings alike. At the community level, Kwanzaa celebrations typically consist of festivals or other community events that include African food, drumming, singing, storytelling, and spoken word performances. Within individual families, Kwanzaa celebrations generally include these same elements, as well as the ceremonial lighting of seven candles known as the *Mishumaa*

Saba, which represent the seven principles of Kwanzaa (we'll say more about these principles later).

In this activity, you'll learn more about Kwanzaa as yet another way to build a sense of connectedness with both your local Black community as well as the larger African diaspora. To begin, start by answering the following questions.

1. How does your community celebrate Kwanzaa? You may find the answer to this question using Google or social media.

   _____

   _____

   _____

2. What parts of the holiday might you like to celebrate or honor?

   _____

   _____

   _____

The Seven Principles of Kwanzaa

The seven principles of Kwanzaa, also known as the *Nguzo Saba*, describe values of African culture that contribute to building and reinforcing community among African Americans (History.com Editors, 2021). You'll find a list of these principles and their descriptions in the following list. On each night of Kwanzaa, the family gathers and a candle representing one of the principles is lit. During this time, the family discusses the principle and its significance. The first candle to be lit is the center candle, which represents umoja, or unity, as this is considered the foundation of success in the community. This candle is black. Placed to the right of the umoja candle are three green candles representing nia (purpose), ujima (collective work and responsibility), and imani (faith). Placed to the left of the umoja candle are three red candles representing kujichagulia (self-determination), ujamaa (cooperative economics), and kuumba (creativity). In this color scheme, black represents our people, red represents our struggle, and green represents the land.

Kwanzaa provides an opportunity for us to intentionally set aside time to honor principles that build and strengthen community. Yet, these principles also represent good practices for everyday life. Therefore, your task in this next part of this activity is to reflect upon how you can honor these principles daily in your life and in your community. The activity ends with space to reflect on how you might celebrate Kwanzaa in December.

❏ **Umoja (Unity):** Maintaining unity as a family, community, and race of people.

How will you demonstrate umoja in your daily life?

_____

_____

_____

❏ **Kujichagulia (Self-Determination):** Defining, naming, creating, and speaking for yourself.

How will you demonstrate kujichagulia in your daily life?

_____

_____

_____

❏ **Ujima (Collective Work and Responsibility):** Building and maintaining our community and solving problems collectively in our community.

How will you demonstrate ujima in your daily life?

_____

_____

_____

❏ **Ujamaa (Cooperative Economics):** Building and maintaining retail and helping businesses to profit in our community.

How will you demonstrate ujamaa in your daily life?

_____

_____

_____

❏ **Nia (Purpose):** Collectively building communities that will restore the greatness of African people.

How will you demonstrate nia in your daily life?

_____

_____

_____

❏ **Kuumba (Creativity):** Finding new, innovative ways to leave communities of African descent in more beautiful and beneficial ways than the community inherited.

How will you demonstrate kuumba in your daily life?

_____

_____

_____

❏ **Imani (Faith):** Belief that through God, family, heritage, our leaders, and others we will see the victory of Africans globally.

How will you demonstrate imani in your daily life?

_____

_____

_____

TABLE 44.1

My Kwanzaa Celebration

My Kwanzaa Celebration						
Umoja	Kujichagulia	Ujima	Ujamaa	Nia	Kuumba	Imani

Kwanzaa is a yearly celebration that takes place each year over seven days from December 26 until January 1. People who celebrate this holiday often take time to share handmade gifts representing each of the seven principles of Kwanzaa over the course of the holiday or on its last day. Sharing gifts can be a fun way to honor loved ones or inspire them to future accomplishments. Use the calendar above to plan how you would like to celebrate Kwanzaa this year and any gifts you would like to share. These gifts should be handmade or inexpensive. Examples include candles, a family photo album, cards, beaded jewelry, or quilts. Remember, the goal is to represent the principles of Kwanzaa in your gift-giving. In case you have forgotten them, below you will find a list of the seven principles along with definitions for each.

Seven Principles of Kwanzaa

- **Umoja (Unity):** Maintaining unity as a family, community, and race of people.

- **Kujichagulia (Self-Determination):** Defining, naming, creating, and speaking for yourself.

- **Ujima (Collective Work and Responsibility):** Building and maintaining our community and solving problems collectively in our community.

- **Ujamaa (Cooperative Economics):** Building and maintaining retail and helping businesses to profit in our community.

- **Nia (Purpose):** Collectively building communities that will restore the greatness of African people.

- **Kuumba (Creativity):** Finding new, innovative ways to leave communities of African descent in more beautiful and beneficial ways than the community inherited.

- **Imani (Faith):** Belief that through God, family, heritage, our leaders, and others we will see the victory of Africans globally.

Black Greek Life

Earlier, we discussed cultural institutions. If you'll recall, cultural institutions are organizations that preserve and protect our cultural heritage. One of the more influential cultural institutions in the Black community is the group of Black Greek-letter fraternities and sororities known as the Divine Nine (D9). This group consists of five historically Black fraternities and four historically Black sororities. Although these fraternities and sororities have different missions and visions, a uniting factor among these organizations is that they all seek to enrich and empower the Black community through service and programming. Accordingly, Black fraternities and sororities play an important role among traditions that keep our cultural heritage and community alive and strong.

Many African Americans have some familiarity with Black fraternities and sororities through personal experience or relatives who are members of these organizations. Others know about them through depictions in popular shows and movies such as *A Different World*, *School Daze*, and *Stomp the Yard*. While based on these depictions there may be a misunderstanding that in order to participate in Black Greek life one must attend college or be a college graduate, the truth is these organizations offer programming for the whole Black community. Moreover, some Black Greek organizations, like Sigma Gamma Rho Sorority Inc., have affiliate groups for youth and non-degreed women that allow for non-degreed women and youth to participate in friendship, support, and community service.

In this activity, you are encouraged to learn more about Black Greek life, as these organizations can be enriching to you and your family. Listed in the following chart is information about these organizations and websites you can use to learn more about them. While you may not be a member of one of these organizations, they often offer community events that are open to the public. Thus, the objective of this activity is to discover which of these organizations are in your community and what opportunities they may have for you to create a sense of community. If you do happen to be a member of one of these organizations, this activity will help you consider how you can use your membership to feel and contribute to a stronger sense of community.

Greek Life in My Community

As mentioned, Black Greek-letter fraternities and sororities offer a variety of programming for the entire community. Table 45.1 lists websites where you can begin to learn more about these organizations. Complete the chart to determine how you can take advantage of this programming. You may want to google the websites for local chapters of these organizations to answer the questions in the last two columns. If you are a member of a fraternity or sorority, you may choose to skip this activity and turn to the next page, as the current activity is more designed for individuals who are not members of Greek organizations.

TABLE 45.1
The Divine Nine

Fraternity/sorority	Greek letters	National website for more information	Are they in my community (Yes or No)	What type of programs do they offer to my community?	How can I participate in these programs?
Alpha Phi Alpha Fraternity, Inc.	ΑΦΑ	https://apa1906.net/			
Alpha Kappa Alpha Sorority, Inc.	ΑΚΑ	https://aka1908.com/			
Kappa Alpha Psi Fraternity, Inc.	ΚΑΨ	https://kappaalphapsi1911.com/			
Omega Psi Phi Fraternity, Inc.	ΩΨΦ	https://oppf.org/			
Delta Sigma Theta Sorority, Inc.	ΔΣΘ	www.deltasigmatheta.org/			
Phi Beta Sigma Fraternity, Inc.	ΦΒΣ	https://phibetasigma1914.org/			
Zeta Phi Beta Sorority, Inc.	ΖΦΒ	https://zphib1920.org/			
Sigma Gamma Rho Sorority, Inc.	ΣΓΡ	https://sgrho1922.org/			
Iota Phi Theta Fraternity, Inc.	ΙΦΘ	www.iotaphitheta.org/			

My Greek Letters

As a member of a Black Greek-letter organization, you have the opportunity to make meaningful contributions to your community through the service and programming your organization offers. The following reflection questions are designed to help you consider the extent to which you participate in this aspect of Greek life and ways you can make this even stronger.

1. How does/did your Greek organization help with the development of who you are as a Black person?

   _____

   _____

   _____

2. In what way does your organization provide you with a sense a community? If it does not, reflect on what could be done to make it feel more like a community? Try and think of things you can personally do to help with this?

   _____

   _____

   _____

3. How does your Greek organization help meet community needs?

   _____

   _____

   _____

4. How could your Greek organization better meet the needs of the Black community? What can you personally do to help meet the needs of your community?

   _____

   _____

   _____

5. How might your Greek organization and the other Divine Nine organizations in your community work collaboratively to make the community in which you serve a better place?

_____

_____

_____

_____

_____

_____

Community Engagement

So far, you've learned that participation in community can contribute to a sense of belonging and empowerment. While these are positive benefits of community engagement, those of us who have been active in our communities know that community involvement also carries a risk for burnout. According to Psychology Today (n.d.), *burnout* can be defined as "a state of emotional, mental, and often physical exhaustion brought on by prolonged or repeated stress." When it occurs, individuals can feel exhausted, cynical, and no longer able to offer work or service they previously loved. One strategy that has been found to be effective for managing burnout is maintaining focus on what it is you love about community involvement. This type of focus and self-reflection helps us to maintain our passion and a sense of connection to the community organizations we value. Moreover, this type of self-reflection can also help us identify community organizations we may have outgrown and that no long serve a purpose in our lives. Use the following reflection questions to examine where you are as it relates to burnout and community engagement.

Reflection Questions

1. List all the communities you are currently involved with (e.g., church community, neighborhood, social/recreational)?

   _____

   _____

   _____

2. What is it about these community organizations you love? What drew you to them?

   _____

   _____

   _____

3. How do these community organizations enrich your life?

   _____

   _____

   _____

4. What does your community involvement or even lack of involvement say about you? Are you experiencing any burnout?

   _____

   _____

   _____

5. Are there ways you would like to be more or less engaged or involved with community organizations? If so, how might you start this process?

   _____

   _____

   _____

Bonus: Self-care is another important strategy for preventing burnout. Next, you will find a list of practices you can adopt to further assist in the prevention of burnout as it relates to community engagement.

- ❏ Take a break
- ❏ Modify your schedule
- ❏ Seek support from others in your community
- ❏ Engage in physical exercise
- ❏ Get enough sleep
- ❏ Eat well
- ❏ Give yourself credit for the work you do—don't minimize your contributions

Community Sense

In the Racial Healing section of this workbook (pp. 21–68), we discussed ways information received through our senses can become part of our trauma, acting as triggers for our negative emotional, behavioral, or physiological responses. A person who is attacked on the street, for example, may remember the smell of the wet sidewalks or the sound of traffic and be taken back to the attack whenever they experience similar smells or sounds. In a comparable way, our senses can also have the reverse effect by calming and soothing physiological responses to trauma (Menakem, 2017). For example, engaging the five senses can help you feel grounded and more connected to reality when experiencing stress or other distressing stimuli. Engaging your senses in a community setting or environment in which you feel secure can have the added benefit of helping you to safely discharge negative energy while also pointing you to individuals or resources that might assist you in this process.

Engaging the Five Senses

In this activity, you will practice engaging your senses in a community setting. We want you to reflect on the things you hear, see, feel, touch, smell, and taste that help you feel secure and create a sense of belonging when you are in your community. For the purpose of this activity, we acknowledge that you may be a part of many different Black communities (e.g., a church community, a sorority/fraternity, or a neighborhood); however, we ask that you pick just one community you are a member of to start with as you complete this activity. You may then go back and answer the prompts for any additional communities to which you belong.

Things I **hear** that help me feel secure in this community.

_____

_____

_____

Things I **see** that help me feel secure in this community.

_____

_____

_____

Things I can **touch** that help me feel secure in this community.

_____

_____

_____

Things I **smell** that help me feel secure in this community.

_____

_____

_____

Things I can **taste** that help me feel secure in this community.

_____

_____

_____

Bonus: As you reflect upon the communities in which you explored your five senses, what patterns or themes do you notice? What helps you feel most secure or happy while in your communities? Examining these questions can be important because your answers might not only assist you in clarifying your needs but may also provide insight into what you should look for as you engage in new community relationships.

Mind, Body, and Soul

In order to have complete wellness, it is important to use the communities to which you are connected to nurture your mind, body, and soul, as holistic health promotes overall wellbeing. Yet, as you may have experienced firsthand, we often experience better health in certain areas of our lives than we do in others. For example, some of us may excel in our careers while we simultaneously struggle with our relationships. This activity is designed to promote greater balance in the various areas of your life by looking at how you can use community to nurture all parts of yourself—mind, body, and soul.

What is Holistic Wellness?

According to researchers Hatfield and Hatfield (1992), *holistic wellness* can be defined as an approach to life that promotes a "conscious and deliberate process by which people are actively involved in enhancing their overall well-being— intellectual, physical, social, emotional, occupational, spiritual" (p. 164). Essentially, holistic wellness refers to an approach to life that (a) recognizes the interconnectedness among all aspects of our humanity and (b) seeks to promote optimal functioning by attending to and nurturing each aspect intentionally. Therefore, holistic wellness also emphasizes the importance of taking responsibility for oneself by creating a sense of wellbeing that is manifested in the person's entire lifestyle (Parmer & Rogers, 1997).

Within the social science literature, while research is limited, holistic wellness has been found to have a significant impact on the overall functioning of African Americans. A study conducted at the University of Iowa, for example, found that mind–body practices focused on meditation and use of a mantra had positive effects on the participants' ability to relax, which in turn reduced blood pressure and the need for blood pressure medication among African Americans with hypertension (Schneider et al., 2005). When considered within the context of community, findings such as this suggest that taking opportunities to nurture the mind, body, and soul in the presence of others with whom we feel a sense of connection and support may have multiplied benefits of promoting health and wellness while also reducing any stigma associated with holistic philosophies.

In what follows, you will find descriptions of the three categories of holistic wellness we've mentioned: mind, body, and soul. After reading each category, create a list identifying how you may integrate practices attending to each of these areas in your own life. As you create your list, think of things that are realistic and fit your lifestyle. You may have to also think of ways you should adjust your lifestyle to nurture these vital parts of yourself.

Mind: Focusing on the mind aspect of holistic wellness includes being aware of things in your community that nurture and support your intellect and mental health needs as a person of color. Some examples of mind-based practices might be a mental health support group or therapist that specializes in or works with people of color, a book club that focuses on reading books centered on Black identity, or engaging in a yoga or meditation group that is designed for people of color.

In the space provided here, list the things in your community you can engage with to support your mind and mental health.

_____

_____

_____

_____

_____

_____

_____

Body: This part of holistic wellness includes the things you can do to support your physical health. Some examples might be finding a doctor of color or a doctor that is culturally sensitive, making sure you attend regular annual and necessary health appointments, joining a Black-owned fitness or exercise program that speaks to your culture (e.g., Zumba), or supporting Black-owned grocery stores and selecting healthy foods.

In the space provided here, list the things in your community you can engage with to support your physical health.

_____

_____

_____

_____

_____

_____

_____

_____

Soul: Finally, this part of holistic wellness reflects the spiritual part of you. It might be connected to a belief in a higher power or it might be connected to the part of you that keeps you grounded and motivated. Some examples of things that might nurture the soul are attending a place of worship, mediation, drumming, or joining a collective yoga group in your community.

In the space provided here, list the things in your community you can engage with to support your soul.

_____

_____

_____

_____

_____

_____

_____

_____

Better Together

In the last few pages of both this part and the entire workbook, we'd like to provide you with an opportunity to reflect on two things: (1) the overall value of community in your life and (2) how you can take what you have learned by completing this workbook to better both yourself and those around you. We've emphasized that having a sense of community can be empowering. Moreover, community can be a gateway to gaining a better understanding of yourself and others, as community provides opportunities to learn things that contribute to a sense of pride and connectedness. Thus, you will find reflection questions designed to help you express final thoughts on the communities to which you belong and what they mean to you. Respond to the questions to put final words to the ultimate meaning of community for you and how we're "better together."

Reflection Questions

1. How are you connected to other people of African descent? What does this connection mean to you?

   _____

   _____

   _____

2. What are the benefits of the Black community having a sense connectedness?

   _____

   _____

   _____

3. Where have you found a sense of community in your local area? How have these communities shaped you?

   _____

   _____

   _____

4. In what ways do you wish you had more connectedness or support from the Black community?

   _____

   _____

   _____

5. How will you use what you have learned from this workbook to better yourself and ultimately the communities that you touch with your life?

   _____

   _____

   _____

Thank You Letter

There is a famous African proverb which states, "It takes a village to raise a child." This proverb means that it takes an entire community of people to grow a child into a healthy and productive individual. As you reflect upon your life from childhood through adulthood, think about the people who have been a part of your village and who have made you who you are today. What are their names? What roles have they had in your life?

In this final activity, you will write a thank you letter to the members of your community who have most impacted your life. Identify at least one person who has helped you become the person you are today and then compose a note acknowledging their importance to you. Be sure to include the following:

❏ What makes them special to you?
❏ For what would you like to thank them?
❏ How you plan to pay it forward in the Black community?

_____

_____

_____

_____

_____

_____

_____

_____

_____

_____

_____

_____

_____

_____

_____

_____

_____

Bonus: If you feel comfortable doing so, give your letter of thanks to the person you wrote about. Letting others know that they are appreciated is an underused kindness in our society. Sharing how you feel can make both you and the person you wrote to feel good.

References

Abrams, J. A., Maxwell, M., Pope, M., & Belgrave, F. Z. (2014). Carrying the world with the grace of a lady and the grit of a warrior: Deepening our understanding of the "Strong Black Woman" Schema. *Psychology of Women Quarterly*, *38*(4), 503–518. https://doi.org/10.1177/0361684314541418

Adejumo, V. (2021). Beyond diversity, inclusion, and belonging. *Leadership*, *17*(1), 62–73. https://doi.org/10.1177/1742715020976202

African Union. (n.d.). The diaspora division. https://au.int/en/diaspora-division

Allan, J. D., Mayo, K., & Michel, Y. (1993). Body size values of White and Black women. *Research in Nursing & Health*, *16*(5), 323–333. https://doi.org/10.1002/nur.4770160503

American Psychiatric Association. (2013). *Diagnostic and statistical manual of mental disorders* (5th ed.). American Psychiatric Association. https://doi.org/10.1176/appi.books.9780890425596

American Psychological Association. (n.d. a). Narrative therapy. In *APA dictionary of psychology*. https://dictionary.apa.org/narrative-therapy

American Psychological Association. (n.d. b). Racial identity. In *APA dictionary of psychology*. https://dictionary.apa.org/racial-identity

American Psychological Association. (n.d. c). Self-efficacy. In *APA dictionary of psychology*. https://dictionary.apa.org/self-efficacy

American Psychological Association. (n.d. d). Visualization. In *APA dictionary of psychology*. https://dictionary.apa.org/visualization

Anderson, L. A. (2019). Rethinking resilience theory in African American families: Fostering positive adaptations and transformative social justice. *Journal of Family Theory & Review, 11*(3), 385–397. https://doi.org/10.1111/jftr.12343

Bailey, T.-K. M., Williams, W. S., & Favors, B. (2014). Internalized racial oppression in the African American community. In E. J. R. David (Ed.), *Internalized oppression: The psychology of marginalized groups* (pp.137–162). Springer Publishing Company, Inc.

Banks, R. R., Eberhardt, J. L., & Ross, L. (2006). Discrimination and implicit bias in a racially unequal society. *California Law Review, 94*(4), 1169–1190.

Barlow, J. N. (2018). Restoring optimal Black mental health and reversing intergenerational trauma in an era of Black Lives Matter. *Biography, 41*(4), 895–908. https://doi.org/10.1353/bio.2018.0084

Barrie, R. E., Langrehr, K., Jerémie-Brink, G., Alder, N., Hewitt, A., & Thomas, A. (2016). Stereotypical beliefs and psychological well-being of African American adolescent girls: Collective self-esteem as a moderator. *Counselling Psychology Quarterly, 29*(4), 423–442. https://doi.org/10.1080/09515070.2015.1129494

Battistin, J. M. (2019). *Exercises to feel calm, stay focused & be your best self: Mindfulness for teens in 10 minutes a day*. Rockridge Press.

Bell, T. P. (2015). Meditative practice cultivates mindfulness and reduces anxiety, depression, blood pressure, and heart rate in a diverse sample. *Journal of Cognitive Psychotherapy, 29*(4), 343–355. https://doi.org/10.1891/0889-8391.29.4.343

Benard, B. (2004). *Resiliency: What we have learned*. WestEd.

Bivens, D. K. (2005). What is internalized racism? *Flipping the Script: White Privilege and Community Building, 1*, 43–51.

Blakesley, B. M. (2016). *African-American and black women's process of learning, unlearning and resisting internalized racism*. Smith Scholar Works.

Boring-Bray, W. (2021). The visualization definition and how it transforms your life. *Better Help*. www.betterhelp.com/advice/visualization/the-visualization-definition-and-how-it-transforms-your-life/

Boston, C., & Warren, S. R. (2017). The effects of belonging and racial identity on urban African American high school students' achievement. *Journal of Urban Learning, Teaching, and Research, 13*, 26–33.

Braveman, P. A., Arkin, E., Proctor, D., Kauh, T., & Holm, N. (2022). Systemic and structural racism: Definitions, examples, health damages, and approaches to dismantling. *Health Affairs, 41*(2),171–178. https://doi.org/10.1377/hlthaff.2021.01394

Britannica. (n.d. a). *African American folktale*. www.britannica.com/art/African-American-folktale

Britannica. (n.d. b). *Griot*. www.britannica.com/art/griot

Britannica. (n.d. c). *Poor People's campaign*. www.britannica.com/topic/Poor-Peoples-March

Britannica Dictionary. (n.d.). Disempower. In *Britannica Dictionary*. https://www.britannica.com/dictionary/disempower

Brooks, M., Wolfgang, J., Adams, J., Armstrong, N., & Cassidy, R. (2020). Using rap music to better understand African American experiences. *Journal of Creativity in Mental Health*, *15*(4), 457–473. https://doi.org/10.1080/15401383.2020.1732251

Brown, D. L. (2008). African American resiliency: Examining racial socialization and social support as protective factors. *Journal of Black Psychology*, *34*(1), 32–48. https://doi.org/10.1177/0095798407310538

Brown, D. L., & Segrist, D. (2016). African American career aspirations: Examining the relative influence of internalized racism. *Journal of Career Development*, *43*(2), 177–189. https://doi.org/10.1177/0894845315586256

Brown, D. L., & Tylka, T. L. (2011). Racial discrimination and resilience in African American young adults: Examining racial socialization as a moderator. *Journal of Black Psychology*, *37*(3), 259–285. https://doi.org/10.1177/0095798410390689

Bryant-Davis, T., Adams, T., Alejandre, A., & Gray, A. A. (2017). The trauma lens of police violence against racial and ethnic minorities. *Journal of Social Issues*, *73*(4), 852–871. https://doi.org/10.1111/josi.12251

Burns, M. A., & Vaughn, K. R. (2021). Race metatheory: Toward a dissolution of a calamitous concept. *Professional Psychology: Research and Practice*, *52*(5), 487–493. http://dx.doi.org/10.1037/pro0000416

Cadaret, M. C., & Speight, S. L. (2018). An exploratory study of attitudes toward psychological help seeking among African American men. *Journal of Black Psychology*, *44*(4), 347–370. https://doi.org/10.1177/0095798418774655

Cameron, N. O., Muldrow, A. F., & Stefani, W. (2018). The weight of things: Understanding African American women's perceptions of health, body image, and attractiveness. *Qualitative Health Research*, *28*(8), 1242–1254. https://doi.org/10.1177/1049732317753588

Carter, R. T. (2007). Racism and psychological emotional injury: Recognizing and assessing race-based traumatic stress. *The Counseling Psychologist*, *35*(1), 13–105. https://doi.org/10.1177/0011000006292033

Carter, R. T., & Forsyth, J. (2010). Reactions to racial discrimination: Emotional stress and help-seeking behaviors. *Psychological Trauma: Theory, Research, Practice, and Policy*, *2*(3), 183–191. https://doi.org/10.1037/a0020102

Carter, R. T., Kirkinis, K., & Johnson, V. E. (2020). Relationships between trauma symptoms and race-based traumatic stress. *Traumatology, 26*(1), 11–18. https://doi.org/10.1037/trm0000217

Case, A. D., & Hunter, C. D. (2012). Counterspaces: A unit of analysis for understanding the role of settings in marginalized individuals' adaptive responses to oppression. *American Journal of Community Psychology, 50*(1–2), 257–270. https://doi.org/10.1007/s10464-012-9497-7

Cherry, K. (2021). *What is self-esteem.* www.verywellmind.com/what-is-self-esteem-2795868

Cleveland Clinic. (n.d.). *Melanin.* https://my.clevelandclinic.org/health/body/22615-melanin

Cobb, M. (2014, May 12). What kind of social change agent are you? *United Way Blog.* www.unitedway.org/blog/what-kind-of-social-change-agent-are-you

Constantine, M. G., Richardson, T. Q., Benjamin, E. M., & Wilson, J. W. (1998). An overview of Black racial identity theories: Current limitations and considerations. *Applied and Preventive Psychology, 7*(2), 95–99. https://doi.org/10.1016/S0962-1849(05)80006-X

Cross, W. E., Jr. (1991). *Shades of Black: Diversity in African-American identity.* Temple University Press.

Cross, W. E., Jr. (1995). The psychology of nigrescence: Revising the Cross model. In J. G. Ponterotto, J. M. Casas, L. A. Suzuki, & C. M. Alexander (Eds.), *Handbook of multicultural counseling* (pp. 93–122). Sage.

DiAngelo, R. (2018). *White fragility: Why it's so hard for White people to talk about racism.* Beacon Press.

Diemer, M. A., Rapa, L. J., Park, C. J., & Perry, J. C. (2017). Development and validation of the Critical Consciousness Scale. *Youth & Society, 49*(4), 461–483. https://doi.org/10.1177/0044118X14538289

Doran, G. T. (1981). There's a S.M.A.R.T. way to write management's goals and objectives. *Management Review, 70*(11), 35–36.

Dunn, C. E., Hood, K. B., & Owens, B. D. (2019). Loving myself through thick and thin: Appearance contingent self-worth, gendered racial microaggressions and African American women's body appreciation. *Body Image, 30,* 121–126. https://doi.org/10.1016/j.bodyim.2019.06.003

Ellin, A. (2021). Brazilian butt lifts surge, despite risks. The New York Times. www.nytimes.com/2021/08/19/style/brazillian-butt-lift-bbl-how-much-risks.html

Endale, L. (2018). The multidimensional model of Black identity and nigrescence theory: A philosophical comparison. *Africology: The Journal of Pan African Studies, 12*(4), 509–524. www.jpanafrican.org/docs/vol12no4/12.4-15-Endale.pdf

Eugene, T. M. (1995). There is a balm in Gilead: Black women and the Black church as agents of a therapeutic community. *Women and Therapy, 16*(2–3), 55–71. https://doi.org/10.1300/J015v16n02_08

Fairbanks, D. J. (2015). *Everyone is African: How science explodes the myth of race.* Prometheus.

Fischer, A. R., & Holz, K. B. (2007). Perceived discrimination and women's psychological distress: The roles of collective and personal self-esteem. *Journal of Counseling Psychology, 54*(2), 154–164. https://doi.org/10.1037/0022-0167.54.2.154

Forsyth, J. M., & Carter, R. T. (2014). Development and preliminary validation of the Racism-Related Coping Scale. *Psychological Trauma: Theory, Research, Practice, and Policy, 6*(6), 632–643. https://doi.org/10.1037/a0036702

Fowers, A., & Wan, W. (2020, June 12). Depression and anxiety spiked among black Americans after George Floyd's death. The Washington Post. www.washingtonpost.com/health/2020/06/12/mental-health-george-floyd-census/

Gates, H. L., Jr., & Tatar, M. (2017). *The annotated African American folktales.* Liveright.

Gentles-Peart, K. (2018). Controlling beauty ideals: Caribbean women, thick bodies, and white supremacist discourse. *Women's Studies Quarterly, 46*(1/2), 199–214.

Gibson, J. D. (1998). Enhancing the motivation of African American middle school adolescents. [Unpublished doctoral dissertation]. University of Akron, OH.

Glasgow, D. (1972). Black power through community control. *Social Work, 17*(3), 59–64. https://doi.org/10.1093/sw/17.3.59

Goodenow, C., & Grady, K. E. (1993). The relationship of school belonging and friends' values to academic motivation among urban adolescent students. *Journal of Experimental Education, 62*(1), 60–71. https://doi.org/10.1080/00220973.1993.9943831

Greenspan, J. (2021). 5 things you may not know about Kwanzaa. As millions of people around the world prepare to celebrate Kwanzaa, explore five things you may not know about this pan-African holiday. www.history.com/news/5-things-you-may-not-know-about-kwanzaa

Gutiérrez, L. M. (1995). Understanding the empowerment process: Does consciousness make a difference? *Social Work Research, 19*(4), 229–237.

Gutiérrez, L., & Creekmore, M. (2013). Cultural institutions and the arts. *Oxford research encyclopedias.* https://doi.org/10.1093/acrefore/9780199975839.013.97

Hackett, G., & Byars, A. M. (1996). Social cognitive theory and the career development of African American women. The Career Development Quarterly, 44(4), 322–340. https://doi.org/10.1002/j.2161-0045.1996.tb00449.x

Hamilton, J. B., Stewart, J. M., Thompson, K., Alvarez, C. Best, N. C., Amoah, K., & Carlton-LaNey, I. B. (2017). Younger African American adults' use of religious songs to manage stressful life events. *Journal of Religion and Health*, 56(1), 329–344. https://doi.org/10.1007/s10943-016-0288-6.

Hatfield, T., & Hatfield, S. R. (1992). As if your life depended on it: Promoting cognitive development to promote wellness. *Journal of Counseling & Development*, 71(2), 164–167. https://doi.org/10.1002/j.1556-6676.1992.tb02192.x

History.com Editors. (2021, December 8). Kwanzaa. www.history.com/topics/holidays/kwanzaa-history

Hsu, T. W., Niiya, Y., Thelwall, M., Ko, M., Knutson, B., & Tsai, J. L. (2021). Social media users produce more affect that supports cultural values, but are more influenced by affect that violates cultural values. *Journal of Personality and Social Psychology*, 121(5), 969–983. https://doi.org/10.1037/pspa0000282

Hughes, E. (2021). "I'm supposed to be thick:" Managing body image anxieties among Black American women. *Journal of Black Studies*, 52(3), 310–330. https://doi.org/10.1177/0021934720972440

Hughes, M., & Demo, D. H. (1989). Self-perceptions of Black Americans: Self-esteem and personal efficacy. *American Journal of Sociology*, 95(1), 132–159. https://doi.org/10.1086/229216

Jacoby, S. F., Rich, J. A., Webster, J. L., & Richmond, T. S. (2020). "Sharing things with people that I don't even know:" Help-seeking for psychological symptoms in injured Black men in Philadelphia. *Ethnicity & Health*, 25(6), 777–795. https://doi.org/10.1080/13557858.2018.1455811

Jagers, R. J., Mustafaa, F. N., & Noel, B. (2017). Cultural integrity and African American empowerment: Insights and practical implications for community psychology. In M. A. Bond, I. Serrano-García, C. B. Keys, & M. Shinn (Eds.), *APA handbook of community psychology: Methods for community research and action for diverse groups and issues* (pp. 459–474). American Psychological Association. https://doi.org/10.1037/14954-027

Jewell, T., & Hoshaw, C. (2021). What is diaphragmatic breathing? www.healthline.com/health/diaphragmatic-breathing

Johnson, A. J. (2020). Examining associations between racism, internalized shame, and self-esteem among African Americans. *Cogent Psychology*, 7(1), Article 1757857. https://doi.org/10.1080/23311908.2020.1757857

Johnson, C. C., Sheffield, K. M., & Brown, R. E. (2018). Mind-body therapies for African-American women at risk for cardiometabolic disease: A systematic review. *Evidence-Based Complementary and Alternative Medicine*. https://doi.org/10.1155/2018/5123217

Johnson, P. D. (2016). Somebodiness and its meaning to African American men. *Journal of Counseling & Development*, 94(3), 333–343. https://doi.org/10.1002/jcad.12089

Johnson, V. E., & Carter, R. T. (2020). Black cultural strengths and psycho-social well-being: An empirical analysis with Black American adults. *Journal of Black Psychology, 46*(1), 55–89. https://doi.org/10.1177/00957 98419889752

Katz, J. H. (1985). The sociopolitical nature of counseling. *The Counseling Psychologist, 13*(4), 615–624. https://doi.org/10.1177/0011000085134005

Kendi, I. X. (2019). *How to be an antiracist.* One World.

Keum, B. T. H., & Cano, M. Á. (2021). Online racism, psychological distress, and alcohol use among racial minority women and men: A multi-group mediation analysis. *American Journal of Orthopsychiatry, 91*(4), 524–530. https://doi.org/10.1037/ort0000553

Kunjufu, J. (1987). *Lessons in history: A celebration in Blackness.* African American Images.

Küver, J. (2017). Cultural heritage as a strategic driver for empower-ment: Exploring the theoretical conjunction. https://heritagestudies.eu/ wp-content/uploads/2017/08/1.3-JKuever_final_clean_13.10.pdf

Lakey, G. (2016, March 9). What role were you born to play in social change? www.opendemocracy.net/en/transformation/what-role-were-you-born-to-play-in-social-change/

Landor, A. M., & Smith, S. M. (2019). Skin-tone trauma: Historical and con-temporary influences on the health and interpersonal outcomes of African Americans. *Perspectives on Psychological Science, 14*(5), 797–815. https:// doi.org/10.1177/1745691619851781

Lebron, C. J. (2017). *The making of Black Lives Matter: A brief history of an idea.* Oxford University Press.

Lee, S. (2000). *The original kings of comedy* [Film]. Paramount Pictures.

Littlejohn-Blake, S. M., & Darling, C. A. (1993). Understanding the strengths of African American families. *Journal of Black Studies, 23*(4), 460–471. https://doi.org/10.1177/002193479302300402

Livingston, J. N., Hughes, K. B., Dawson, D., Williams, A., Mohabir, J. A., Eleanya, A., Cliette, G., & Brandon, D. (2017). Feeling no ways tired: A resurgence of activism in the African American community. *Journal of Black Studies, 48*(3), 279–304. https://doi.org/10.1177/0021934717690526

Lord, J., & Hutchison, P. (1993). The process of empowerment: Implications for theory and practice. *Canadian Journal of Community Mental Health, 12*(1), 5–22. www.johnlord.net/web_documents/process_of_empowerment.pdf

Mandela, N. (1995). *Long walk to freedom: The autobiography of Nelson Mandela.* Back Bay Books.

Maxwell, M., Brevard, J., Abrams, J., & Belgrave, F. (2015). What's color got to do with it? Skin color, skin color satisfaction, racial identity, and internalized racism among African American college students. *Journal of Black Psychology, 41*(5), 438–461. https://doi.org/10.1177/009579841 4542299

McCallum, C. (2017). Giving back to the community: How African Americans envision utilizing their PhD. *Journal of Negro Education, 86*(2), 138–153.

Menakem, R. (2017). *My grandmother's hands: Racialized trauma and the pathway to mending our hearts and bodies.* Central Recovery Press.

Mohatt, N. V., Thompson, A. B., Thai, N. D., Tebes, J. K. (2014). Historical trauma as public narrative: A conceptual review of how history impacts present-day health. *Social Science & Medicine, 106*, 128–136. https://doi. org/10.1016/j.socscimed.2014.01.043

Nadal, K. L. (2018). *Microaggressions and traumatic stress: Theory, research, and clinical treatment.* American Psychological Association.

Neff, K. D. (2016). "The Self-Compassion Scale is a valid and theoretically coherent measure of self-compassion": Erratum. *Mindfulness, 7*(4), 1009. https://doi.org/10.1007/s12671-016-0560-6

Nelson, T., Shahid, N. N., & Cardemil, E. V. (2020). Do I really need to go and see somebody? Black Women's perceptions of help-seeking for depression. *Journal of Black Psychology, 46*(4), 263–286. https://doi.org/10.1177/00957 98420931644

Nembhard, J. M. (2008). Alternative economics—A missing component in the African American studies curriculum: Teaching public policy and demo-cratic community economics to Black undergraduate students. *Journal of Black Studies, 38*(5), 758–782. https://doi.org/10.1177/0021934707310294

Neville, H. A., Awad, G. H., Brooks, J. E., Flores, M. P., & Bluemel, J. (2013). Color-blind racial ideology: Theory, training, and measurement implications in psychology. *American Psychologist, 68*(6), 455–466. https:// doi.org/10.1037/a0033282

Neville, H. A., & Cross, W. E., Jr. (2017). Racial awakening: Epiphanies and encounters in Black racial identity. *Cultural Diversity and Ethnic Minority Psychology, 23*(1), 102–108. https://doi.org/10.1037/cdp0000105

Ngugi wa Thiong'o (1986). *Decolonising the mind: The politics of language in African literature.* East African Educational Publishers.

Nix, E. (2021). What is Juneteenth? Juneteenth commemorates the effective end of slavery in the United States. www.history.com/news/what-is-jun eteenth

Obear, K. (2017). *But I'm not racist! Tools for well-meaning Whites.* The Difference Press.

Okeke-Adeyanju, N., Taylor, L. C., Craig, A. B., Smith, R. E., Thomas, A., Boyle, A. E., & DeRosier, M. E. (2014). Celebrating the strengths of Black youth: Increasing self-esteem and implications for prevention. *The Journal of Primary Prevention, 35*(5), 357–369. https://10.1007/s10935-014-0356-1

Osa, M. L., & Kelly, N. R. (2021). Experiences of discrimination are associated with drive for muscularity among African American men. *Psychology of Men & Masculinities, 22*(2), 365–374. https://doi.org/10.1037/men0000287

Parham, T. A., & Helms, J. E. (1985). Attitudes of racial identity and self-esteem of Black students: An exploratory investigation. *Journal of College Student Personnel, 26*(2), 143–147.

Parmer, T., & Rogers, T. (1997). Religion and health: Holistic wellness from the perspective of two African American church denominations. *Counseling and Values, 42*(1), 55–67. https://doi.org/10.1002/j.2161-007X.1997.tb00953.x

Pascoe, E. A., & Richman, L. S. (2009). Perceived discrimination and health: A meta-analytic review. *Psychological Bulletin, 135*(4), 531–554. https://doi.org/10.1037/a0016059

Patterson, K. L. (2004). A longitudinal study of African American women and the maintenance of a healthy self-esteem. *Journal of Black Psychology, 30*(3), 307–328. https://doi.org/10.1177/0095798404266065

Payne, J. S. (2012). Influence of race and symptom expression on clinicians' depressive disorder identification in African American men. *Journal of the Society for Social Work and Research, 3*(3), 162–177. https://doi.org/10.5243/jsswr.2012.11

Pieterse, A. L., Todd, N. R., Neville, H. A., & Carter, R. T. (2012). Perceived racism and mental health among Black American adults: A meta-analytic review. *Journal of Counseling Psychology, 59*(1), 1–9. https://doi.org/10.1037/a0026208

Polanco-Roman, L., Danies, A., & Anglin, D. M. (2016). Racial discrimination as race-based trauma, coping strategies, and dissociative symptoms among emerging adults. *Psychological Trauma: Theory, Research, Practice, and Policy, 8*(5), 609–617. https://doi.org/10.1037/tra0000125

Prilleltensky, I., & Gonick, L. (1996). Polities change, oppression remains: On the psychology and politics of oppression. *Political Psychology, 17*(1), 127–148. https://doi.org/10.2307/3791946

Psychology Today. (n.d.). *Burnout.* www.psychologytoday.com/us/basics/burnout

Pyke, K. D. (2010). What is internalized racial oppression and why don't we study it? Acknowledging racism's hidden injuries. *Sociological Perspectives, 53*(4), 551–572. https://doi.org/10.1525/sop.2010.53.4.551

Ramsden, P. (2017). Vicarious trauma, PTSD and social media: Does watching graphic videos cause trauma? *Journal of Depression and Anxiety.* www.longdom.org/proceedings/vicarious-trauma-ptsd-and-social-media-does-watching-graphic-videos-cause-trauma-37421.html

Rankin, K. (2016, June 27). Watch the BET Awards Speech That Sparked #JesseWilliamsAppreciationDay. *Colorlines.* www.colorlines.com/articles/watch-bet-awards-speech-sparked-jessewilliamsappreciationday

Reddix, J. (1974). *A voice crying in the wilderness: The memoirs of Jacob L. Reddix.* University Press of Mississippi.

Roberts, D. (2012). *Fatal invention: How science, politics, and big business re-create race in the twenty-first century.* The New Press.

Rosenberg, M. (1979). *Conceiving the self.* Basic Books.

Savali, K. W. (2014). Dr. Martin L. King Jr.: 'I'm Black and I'm Beautiful' [VIDEO]. https://newsone.com/2843703/dr-martin-l-king-jr-im-black-and-im-beautiful-video/

Schiele, J. H. (2005). Cultural oppression and the high-risk status of African Americans. *Journal of Black Studies, 35*(6), 802–826. https://doi.org/10.1177/0021934704265560

Schneider, R. H., Alexander, C. N., Staggers, F., Orme-Johnson, D. W., Rainforth, M., Salerno, J. W., Sheppard, W., Castillo-Richmond, A., Barnes, V. A., & Nidich, S. I. (2005). A randomized controlled trial of stress reduction in African Americans treated for hypertension for over one year. *American journal of hypertension, 18*(1), 88–98. https://doi.org/10.1016/j.amjhyper.2004.08.027

Scott, E. (2020). Body scan meditation: Release tension with this targeted meditation technique. https://nursing.rutgers.edu/wp-content/uploads/2020/07/Body-Scan-Meditation.docx

Shipp, P. L. (1983). Counseling Blacks: A group approach. *The Personnel and Guidance Journal, 62,* 108–111.

Sidanius, J., & Pratto, F. (1999). *Social dominance: An intergroup theory of social hierarchy and oppression.* Cambridge University Press. https://doi.org/10.1017/CBO9781139175043

Simmons, C., Worrell, F., & Berry, J. (2008). Psychometric properties of scores on three black racial identity scales. *Assessment, 15*(3), 259–276. https://doi.org/10.1177/1073191108314788

Smedley, A. (1997). Origins of "race." *Anthropology News, 38*(8), 1–52. https://doi.org/10.1111/an.1997.38.8.52

Smedley, A. (1999). *Race in North America: Origin and evolution of a worldview* (2nd ed.). Westview Press.

Smedley, A., & Smedley, B. D. (2005). Race as biology is fiction, racism as a social problem is real: Anthropological and historical perspectives on the social construction of race. *American Psychologist, 60*(1), 16–26. https://doi.org/10.1037/0003-066X.60.1.16

Smithsonian. (n.d.). Roots of African American music. www.si.edu/spotlight/african-american-music/roots-of-african-american-music

Solórzano, D., Ceja, M., & Yosso, T. (2000). Critical race theory, racial microaggressions, and campus racial climate: The experiences of African American college students. *Journal of Negro Education, 69*(1-2), 60–73.

Steele, J. M. (2020). A CBT approach to internalized racism among African Americans. *International Journal for the Advancement of Counselling, 42*(3), 217–233. https://doi.org/10.1007/s10447-020-09402-0

Steele, J. M., & Lee, T. K. (2022). Recognizing and addressing microaggressions in addiction treatment groups: An integrated approach. Journal of Addictions & Offender Counseling. Advance online publication. https://doi.org/10.1002/jaoc.12103

Steele, J. M., & Newton, C. S. (2022). Culturally adapted cognitive behavior therapy as a model to address internalized racism among African American clients. *Journal of Mental Health Counseling, 44*(2), 98–116. https://doi.org/10.17744/mehc.44.2.01

Stephens, D. P., & Few, A. L. (2007). The effects of images of African American women in hip hop on early adolescents' attitudes toward physical attractiveness and interpersonal relationships. *Sex Roles: A Journal of Research, 56*(3-4), 251–264. https://doi.org/10.1007/s11199-006-9145-5

Substance Abuse and Mental Health Services Administration. (2020). 2019 National Survey on Drug Use and Health: African Americans. www.samhsa.gov/data/report/2019-nsduh-african-americans

Sue, D. W., Alsaidi, S., Awad, M. N., Glaeser, E., Calle, C. Z., & Mendez, N. (2019). Disarming racial microaggressions: Microintervention strategies for targets, White allies, and bystanders. *American Psychologist, 74*(1), 128–142. http://dx.doi.org/10.1037/amp0000296

Sue, D. W., Calle, C. Z., Mendez, N., Alsaidi, S., & Glaeser, E. (2021). *Microintervention strategies: What you can do to disarm and dismantle individual and systemic racism and bias.* John Wiley & Sons, Inc.

Sue, D. W., & Sue, D. (2016). *Counseling the culturally diverse* (7th ed.). John Wiley & Sons, Inc.

Sullivan, J., Wilton, L., & Apfelbaum, E. P. (2021). Adults delay conversations about race because they underestimate children's processing of race. *Journal of Experimental Psychology: General, 150*(2), 395–400. https://doi.org/10.1037/xge0000851

Sweeton, J. (2017). To heal trauma, work with the body: It's not all just in your head. *Psychology Today.* www.psychologytoday.com/us/blog/workings-well-being/201708/heal-trauma-work-the-body

Taie, S., & Goldring, R. (2020). Characteristics of Public and Private Elementary and Secondary School Teachers in the United States: Results From the 2017–18 National Teacher and Principal Survey First Look (NCES 2020-142). U.S. Department of Education. National Center for Education Statistics. https://nces.ed.gov/pubsearch/pubsinfo.asp?pubid=2020142.

Talleyrand, R. M., Gordon, A. D., Daquin, J. V., & Johnson, A. J. (2017). Expanding our understanding of eating practices, body image, and appearance in African American women: A qualitative study. *Journal of Black Psychology*, *43*(5), 464–492. https://doi.org/10.1177/0095798416649086

Tatum, B. D. (2017). *Why are all the Black kids sitting together in the cafeteria? And other conversations about race.* Basic Books.

Tawa, J., Ma, R., & Katsumoto, S. (2016). "All Lives Matter:" The cost of color-blind racial attitudes in diverse social networks. *Race and Social Problems*, *8*(2), 196–208. https://doi.org/10.1007/s12552-016-9171-z

Tedeschi, R. G., & Kilmer, R. P. (2005). Assessing strengths, resilience, and growth to guide clinical interventions. *Professional Psychology: Research and Practice*, *36*(3), 230–237. https://doi.org/10.1037/0735-7028.36.3.230

Terry, C. L., Sr., Flennaugh, T. K., Blackmon, S. M., & Howard, T. C. (2014). Does the "Negro" "still" need separate schools? Single-sex educational settings as critical race counterspaces. *Urban Education*, *49*(6), 666–697.

Thomas, A. (2017). The hate u give. HarperCollins.

Tucker, C., Dixon, A., & Griddine, K. (2010). Academically successful African American male urban high school students' experiences of mattering to others at School. *Professional School Counseling*, *14*(2), 135–145. https://doi.org/10.1177/2156759X1001400202

Tuwe, K. (2016). The African oral tradition paradigm of storytelling as a methodological framework: Employment experiences for African communities in New Zealand. In: African Studies Association of Australasia and the Pacific (AFSAAP) Proceedings of the 38th AFSAAP Conference: 21st Century Tensions and Transformation in Africa. Deakin University.

Tyson, E., Detchkov, K., Eastwood, E., Carver, A., & Sehr, A. (2013). Therapeutically and socially relevant themes in hip-hop: A comprehensive analysis of a selected sample of songs. In S. Hadley & G. Yancey (Eds.), *Therapeutic uses of rap and hip-hop* (pp. 99–118). Routledge.

Umaña-Taylor, A. J., Quintana, S. M., Lee, R. M., Cross, W. E., Rivas-Drake, D., Schwartz, S. J., Syed, M., Yip, T., Seaton, E., & Ethnic and Racial Identity in the 21st Century Study Group. (2014). Ethnic and racial identity during adolescence and into young adulthood: An integrated conceptualization. *Child Development*, *85*(1), 21–39. https://doi.org/10.1111/cdev.12196

Ungar, M. (2013). Resilience, trauma, context, and culture. *Trauma, Violence, & Abuse*, *14*(3), 255–266. https://doi.org/10.1177/1524838013487805

U.S. Census Bureau. (2018). Income and poverty in the United States: 2018. www.census.gov/content/dam/Census/library/publications/2019/demo/p60-266.pdf

Vandiver, B. J., Fhagen-Smith, P. E., Cokley, K. O., Cross, W. E., Jr., & Worrell, F. C. (2001). Cross's nigrescence model: From theory to scale to theory. *Journal of Multicultural Counseling and Development, 29*(3), 174–200. https://doi.org/10.1002/j.2161-1912.2001.tb00516.x

Versey, H. S., Cogburn, C. C., Wilkins, C. L., & Joseph, N. (2019). Appropriated racial oppression and its role for health in whites and blacks. *Social Science & Medicine, 230*, 295–302. https://doi.org/10.1016/j.socsci med.2019.03.014

Waiting to Exhale. (2022, May 30). In *Wikipedia.* https://en.wikipedia.org/wiki/Waiting_to_Exhale

Wald, J., Taylor, S., Asmundson, G. J., Jang, K. L., & Stapleton, J. (2006). *Literature review of concepts: Psychological resiliency* (No. DRDC-CR-2006-073). British Columbia University.

Watson, L. B., Ancis, J. R., White, D. N., & Nazari, N. (2013). Racial identity buffers African American women from body image problems and disordered eating. *Psychology Women Quarterly, 37*(3), 337–350. https://doi.org/10.1177/0361684312474799

Watson, N. N., & Hunter, C. D. (2015). Anxiety and depression among African American women: The costs of strength and negative attitudes toward psychological help-seeking. *Cultural Diversity and Ethnic Minority Psychology, 21*(4), 604–612. https://doi.org/10.1037/cdp0000015

Watson-Singleton, N. N., Black, A. R., & Spivey, B. N. (2019). Recommendations for a culturally-responsive mindfulness-based intervention for African Americans. *Complementary Therapy in Clinical Practice, 34*, 132–138. https://doi.org/10.1016/j.ctcp.2018.11.013

West, N. M. (2019). In the company of my sister-colleagues: Professional counterspaces for African American women student affairs administrators. *Gender and Education, 31*(4), 543–559. https://doi.org/10.1080/09540 253.2018.1533926

Whitlock, J., Mai, T., Call, M., & Van Epps, J. (2021, February 24). *How to practice self-compassion for resilience and well-being.* https://accelerate.uof uhealth.utah.edu/resilience/how-to-practice-self-compassion-for-resilie nce-and-well-being

Wolkin, J. (2016, June 15). *The science of trauma, mindfulness, and PTSD.* https://braincurves.com/2016/06/17/repost-the-science-of-trauma-mind fulness-and-ptsd/

Workneh, L. (2022, January/February). The rise of the Black is Beautiful revolution. *Essence*, 80–83.

Worrell, F. C., Cross, W. E., Jr., & Vandiver, B. J. (2001). Nigrescence theory: Current status and challenges for the future. *Journal of Multicultural Counseling and Development, 29*(3), 201–213. https://doi.org/10.1002/j.2161-1912.2001.tb00517.x

References

Yap, S. C. Y., Settles, I. H., & Pratt-Hyatt, J. S. (2011). Mediators of the relationship between racial identity and life satisfaction in a community sample of African American women and men. *Cultural Diversity and Ethnic Minority Psychology, 17*(1), 89–97. https://doi.org/10.1037/a0022535

Zhang, Y., Dixon, T. L., & Conrad, K. (2009). Rap music videos and African American women's body image: The moderating role of ethnic identity. *Journal of Communication, 59*(2), 262–278. https://doi.org/10.1111/j.1460-2466.2009.01415.x

Zimmerman, M. A. (1995). Psychological empowerment: Issues and illustrations. *American Journal of Community Psychology, 23*(5), 581–599. https://doi.org/10.1007/BF0250698